THE WAY OF MERLYN
The Male Path in Wicca

Acknowledgements

I would like to acknowledge the story-telling abilities of Kathryn Matthews; the members of the Order of Stellar Fire; the members of the Coven of Crystalglade; Colleen for her valued advice on Dragons; The Celtic Studies Department of Sydney University.

I would not have attempted this work had it not been for the dedicated harassment of Aaron, High Priest of the Coven of Crystalglade and father to two of my three children.

I wish also to acknowledge the inspired writings of the following authors: Dolores Ashcroft-Nowicki, Marion Bradley, Kenneth Flint, Christine Hartley, Gareth Knight, Alan Richardson, Lewis Spence.

THE WAY OF MERLYN

THE MALE PATH IN WICCA

LY WARREN-CLARKE & KATHRYN MATTHEWS

PRISM · UNITY

Published in Great Britain 1990 by
PRISM PRESS
2 South Street, Bridport,
Dorset DT6 3NQ

and

Distributed in the USA by
Avery Publishing Group,
120 Old Broadway,
Garden City Park,
NY 11040

Published in Australia by
UNITY PRESS
Lindfield
NSW 2070

ISBN 1 85327 041 5

Cover illustration: Linda Garland

Typeset by Maggie Spooner Typesetting, London.
Printed by The Guernsey Press Ltd, The Channel Islands.

Contents

This whole book is a Pattern, a Maze. Each section will entwine about itself and hold the truth to many Puzzles. Not all who read it will understand the Pattern and so will not gain — they will probably just read it!

For those of you who seek to understand the Pattern and who can travel its Pathways we shout — to Earth, Moon, Sun and Star — 'All hail and well met! We honour you, Priest of the Ancient Way! Welcome home!'

This is the Path of the Solar/Earth Priest, but not alone — always do the Priestesses of the Moon dance with the same music.

We would first and foremost like to dedicate this work to the lasting patience of Michael, Archangelic Lord of Fire and holder of the Staff of Merlyn on our behalf, and secondly to our own Priests, and to the Fathers, Brothers, Sons and Lovers of a thousand lifetimes — and those who are yet to be.

Blessed be.

Ly and Kathryn.

Prologue

He lies upon his bed with his arm flung over his eyes, thinking deeply about his chosen Path and his love of the old Gods and about who he is and just where the Dream began.

He breathes deeply, rhythmically, attuning his racing mind to the music of his own body to still the thoughts that interfere with his quest.

He seems to sleep . . . not many would know that he does not.

He sees before his inner eyes the Tunnel of Time. He projects his spirit towards this place and finds himself being drawn down and backwards, way, way back to the very dawn of Christendom in a land of emerald green and ageless beauty.

He finds himself flying low over rolling hills and moorlands, circling freely over forests and small hamlets of country folk, over manor and mere heading towards the inevitable destiny of one man.

The mists settle over the land in rolling plumes of wraith-like form that obscure all before him.

He slows as he closes the distance between his world and theirs. The timelessness of a winter night is silent; not even the sound of the hawk can be heard through the thickening pall. He hears muffled sounds from the marshland below him and he comes to ground level where the mist is not so thick, but moving, steadily shapeshifting as it swirls around the mire.

There! Just ahead is the man on horseback! He carries a lantern to pick his way through this desolate place.

The boy takes up the story of what he sees upon his Inner Quest . . .

'I swoop slowly and land as a mist upon the horse's rump. I

attune to the man upon its back — he thinks of naught. He must not lose his thoughts upon any other theme than that of following the almost imperceptible path through this empty place.

No life here. The lights of a thousand lost souls glint through the mist to remind him of his peril, but he hesitates not and heeds not their warnings. His Destiny burns within his soul that would destroy him were it not fulfilled.

I see him clearly by the light of the lantern; outlined with the ravages of many an unslept night, he is gaunt. His jaw twitches with his effort and his eyes are haunted by his Dream. He is a physically powerful man, bull-like in his build with lantern clenched vice-like in his hand. His clothing is simple; thonging criss-crosses the furs about his calves and woollen leggings as thick as mail about his thighs. His jerkin is the skin of a wolf snared in some past day and his cloak is russet and of heavy woven wool that hangs limply along the side of his mare. He wears a hood of leather but his hair lays in dark, tangled rivulets down his back. His beard is full and obscures the grim line of his mouth which is set in an attitude of determination, rarely seen in one of my day.

The length, thus far, of his journey lays heavily upon him and his shoulders are bent forward with fatigue . . . but he may not stop until he is past this dreadful place.

Hour upon hour we move, well into the midnight, until at last the mare raises her head and snorts as she stumbles onto the grassland. We travel slowly, still, until the rider is certain of his bearings, then he roars with triumph and we are off, flying like the wind, as the plain thunders beneath us!

We slow as dawn creeps above the horizon in a washed-out blur, and horse and rider, sweating at their efforts, breathe deeply at the sight. We come at length to a copse of trees into which we walk. The rider dismounts and leads his beloved mare into the depths. There, a stream, cool and deep, at which the mare and rider might drink. He then leads his horse to graze beneath the oaks and peers around, furtively, to guess that none come here often and he may have peace for a few hours during which he will rest. I know not why, but know it I do, that he wishes to be seen by no-one, so he rides by night and hides by day so that none may know he is abroad.

He unsaddles the mare, crooning to her as he does so, and rubs her down with the blanket from beneath the saddle. A smile crosses his face and a look that stirs my soul with its intensity and passion. His task done, he proceeds to prepare a small fire over which he roasts potatoes and a strip of dried meat. He draws from his pouch a leather flask from which he quaffs deeply. Having eaten his simple meal he stamps the fire and curls within his cloak to sleep away the daylight hours: and so I watch . . .

At one point I rise above the trees to seek and ascertain his safety, for although he is furtive and afeared of notice I feel for him in his quest almost as though it were my own, and my heart reaches out to the strength within him and I know he would harm none without good cause. I know not how I would rouse him should danger approach, but there is no farm or village within distance so I fear not for him.

I return to find him turning about restlessly within his sleep, the Dream causing much mumbling and sighing within him; and so it is for a few hours more until he is awakened by his own shouts. Sweat beads upon his face and he stands and removes his hood and cloak, and walks to the stream to wash himself and so lose the Dreaming. He again lights the fire and draws from his pouch a large cup which he fills from the stream. He brews a draught of strong herbs to help him to wakefulness for the long night ahead.

His journey will be done, thus far, on this night — at least where riding is concerned; the journey is just beginning of the rest of his life, the end of which is assured in his mind. There is no escaping what he so earnestly seeks but what he as earnestly dreads, for it is unclear to him what ventures will befall him between the present moment and his eventual death.

He stamps the fire and covers its remains with dirt and brambles so that none may know that any had passed this way. He calls to the mare — "Billah!", he calls and the mare comes from her grazing by the stream. He saddles her and attaches his pouch to his belt. He dons hood and cloak and mounts, I behind him. We move slowly through the trees in the direction of the setting sun. We reach the edge of the woods and wait.

When the night is black we ride; hour upon hour do we ride. This night is clear and he watches the stars for his bearings. Sometimes we walk his horse, sometimes it almost seems that we fly. Up ahead the Moon grows full and high, lighting our way. Ahead I see monolithic rocks rising to the night sky and the mist of ocean reaches all about us. The tang of salt is in his nose and his nostrils flare and his eyes widen with that same unseeing passion that I saw in the woods. We approach the cliffs and I hear the roar of waves thrashing upon the rocks below as if trying to draw all within themselves. A wild place is this! I see through his eyes the vast expanse of inky blackness within each rock's shadow and which is also the sea over which the Moon glows, causing a pathway between Herself and the things beneath the waters.

He stops to light the lantern for the path is rough and Billah troubles with each step. The Rider sighs and lays his head upon his arm before raising himself straight within the saddle. "It is now," he whispers, "We wait and seek no more! As known, I have arrived!" He looks ahead to a rocky outcrop like a finger upon the sea. I see naught and do not understand.

We ride hard then, sparks flying from the horse's hooves upon the granite way. As we approach the peninsula I see a faint glow, as if from a lantern. The Rider slows and throws his own light over the cliff; he is wary and seeks to approach unseen. He dismounts and walks towards the glow. I see a small cottage almost buried, so deeply within the overhang of the cliffs was it built, like a tiny fortress against the wild winds and sea. A lonelier spot I have never known . . .

The Rider's face is set like stone and I cannot perceive his thoughts. He walks with dignity, as if to his death.

We come at length to the door, of massive proportion compared to the size of the cottage. The Rider hesitates not but bangs his fist upon it, a sigh upon his lips. There is a wait, then

4

comes a woman's voice saying: "Who comes?"

"I am called Llugh!" he calls. There is a laugh from within and the door is swung wide. There stands a girl of about twenty years, dressed in male attire but with wild copper hair cascading down her back.

"You are doubly welcome, Llugh, and thrice! We have waited long for your coming!"

"I knew it to be true!" Llugh replies, although he smiles not, "Was it you who called me here?"

"It was your own Dream, Llugh, and not of our doing. Enter, I shall tether the mount and see her well."

"What Name have you?" he asks, without moving; but she just smiles and shakes her head and again bids him enter.

The room is dark save for the lantern in the window and the fire in the hearth. Llugh sees that only the first of the cottage is man-hewn and that the rest is of solid rock formed from the depths of the cliff. A man stands from his chair beside the fire. He is straight of frame and as tall as an Elm, but the whiteness of his beard and hair tell of his age. His hair falls to his shoulders and takes the fire-glow with it. He wears a robe of heavy dove-grey wool and as he moves towards Llugh he smiles. Llugh sees great love in the smile, but as he looks to the eyes of the old man he flinches at their blackness and depths ... there is un-fathomable power within them as though they had perceived the passing of time from its very conception and had learned from the travel all that had been there to learn.

"I've missed you, Llugh! Blessed be!" the old man says as if he knew the younger man well. He takes Llugh's arm and leads him to stand before the fire. "We have known that you would come!" He laughs with obvious glee.

"Who is the woman? By all the Gods, who are you?" demands Llugh, as, although this whole thing excites him, he fears it also and is tired of the mystery that has haunted him waking and sleeping.

"She is Who I am, and Who you are to become!" replies the old man.

"Her Name?"

"Call Her Morgana and She will answer you!"

"And you, Sir, what be your Name?" Llugh asks again.

"Merlyn."

"Any why am I here, Merlyn?"

"To learn, Llugh, the Secret of Life and Fire! To take Morgana to your Soul and mould tomorrow with all of my yesterdays!" he replies.

"Apprentice? Is that it? Apprentice shall I be?"

"Aye, Llugh, Apprentice shall you be!" laughs Merlyn.

I return, now, through time, to dwell upon what I have seen. I love Him with whom I rode, for He is me. I love Her, for the Goddess is within Her. And of Merlyn? Well, I shall say hello for you when I see Him on the morrow!'

Introduction

This work is intended as a sequel to *The Way of the Goddess*. You will find the specific disciplines and fundamental training techniques within its pages, and I must advise any who read this text to prepare in response to your Magical Will by utilising the training therein.

Many have said that *The Way of the Goddess* was a book written for women only, but in this they are mistaken, as it is purely the fact that I am a woman and Priestess that makes it seem so. This text should, perhaps, be written by a Priest of our Art, but as none have done so and the women are waiting for you, we shall do so on their behalf! (How's that for a challenge?)

Witchcraft reinforces in our society the honour and love of the Goddess, and hence all women. It is also a process of integrating both male and female polarities, not only within the self but also, through mutual acknowledgement of God within each man and Goddess within each woman, the spirit of Duality within the whole of Nature, the nature of Opposites throughout all things where there is Life (and where isn't there Life?), and acting upon this knowledge for the continued survival of Gaia and all who dwell upon Her.

We feel that it is the denial of all that we fear, the denial of our Wildselves, the denial of the inevitability of change and death that blocks us from fulfilling our true Destinies. To understand that we are all as multi-faceted as jewels and that these jewels are divine is to set ourselves free from the expectations of others and, as a consequence, we can get on with the important work of fulfilling our parts in the Destiny of the Evolving Whole.

Women who choose Initiation into Wicca have the knowledge of the many Faces of the Goddess at their fingertips — they need only to seek the Faces of the Triple Goddess and they will be confronted with Her from every recorded pantheon of history, thanks to the work of many over the past two or three decades. Priestesses will seek to integrate these Faces at all times within everything they think, do, say and feel; they have the phases of the Moon to guide them, the cycles of their own bodies and, through the countless years of suppression, the power to bring forth their true individuality into not only relationships but society as a whole.

Now, we are not certain that the problems we have in Australia are worldwide and we would be interested to learn if this is so; here, with vast distances between many of us, the problems of the Priestesses of Wicca are obvious. There are more women than men training in Witchcraft and that training involves its own unique and fundamental difficulties; we are not Dianic Witches but work with both a God and a Goddess. The women, when properly trained, are among the strongest, woman-proud creatures that you would ever have the honour of knowing. There are more per coven than men, and in many instances where men do seek Initiation they are either egoistic, overbearing or lost to the impact of their own power by a society that has conditioned their greater passions out of them. Much of this we blame on our own culture, as the Rite of Passage does not exist for men and they are under constant pressure from that same culture to conform to the attitudes of other men, usually to their detriment (as most men do not understand the ways of women sufficiently to interrelate through mutual respect of our intrinsic differences), and many of these same applicants are put on immediate defensive by these well-trained Priestesses.

The men who do seek Initiation into the Priesthood of Wicca have one plus that holds them in good stead — they *know* what they want to give, and it is very much the right of the Goddess to work through Her women to show the men how they can give it whilst gaining, in balanced return, all the rights available to them through both honouring Her and finding their God within themselves.

We are the Children of the Gods, and as such we adore the spirit of all things and seek to interweave our lives with the

Pattern of the Evolving Whole, but unlike other religions we seek to do this by answering to the call of the Wildness in ourselves as well as the Enlightened.

We are of the Earth (Gaia), our bodies are physical, we learn all about birth, life and death and seek to give each of these Passages its due respect; turning one's face 'heavenwards' and denying the physical plane and all that it signifies is the root of disintegration that we see occurring on our planet right now. This disintegration must not be allowed to persist; only by seeking, through our natural inheritance, to work *with* the forces of Duality will we have a common purpose, i.e. to live here and now to our greatest potential and to then give it away to the Forces that we worship; we do not need to understand the purpose, only to work within it.

Kathryn and I have brought to you symbolic Legends and practical disciplines that will open the doors of the men to their freeflowing Priesthoods. The workings herein are specifically masculine, as the women of Wicca are after their balancing agent; we have our own work to do.

Do the work. We will know you when we meet you!

Part One:
The Erl-King and You

'The night is late and wild, as a father and his small son are thundering on horseback through a dark and forbidding forest. The boy sits before his father, held close by the man's strong and loving arms. The deep woods seem to press closely all around them as they gallop through the howling winds and driving rain towards home, and safety. The boy is afraid, his face white and tense.

"Father," he cries, "See before us! 'Tis the Erl-King, in crown and shroud; he beckons me, Father, he beckons, me!" "Peace, my son," replies the man, "it is the mist around the trees, naught else."

On and on they ride, the father's grip tightening around his beloved boy. Again and again the lad cries out, becoming more terrified with each passing moment. He begs his father to believe him, as the Erl-King whispers low in his ear, first cajolingly, then threateningly, and still the man seeks to soothe his son and calm his fears. Spurring the horse on to even greater speed the boy's father shudders as he feels his son's small body tremble and hears him whimper in fear. Finally, with home almost in sight, the boy screams in terror: "He has me, Father! Ah, his touch is icy cold and cruel! Father . . . Father!"

In an agony of dread the man at last reaches his door to find the little boy dead in his arms.'

* * *

This powerful story is the subject of a famous piece by Schubert, from a poem by Goethe, that has arrested the attention of the hearts and minds of its hearers since it was first written. If you were to think that the story has three main characters you would be wrong. It has only one: you.

11

The father is your rational, thinking self; your conscious self, and the self that you normally present to the world. The child is the 'little boy' in you, the self which feels insecurities and vulnerabilities that the father is afraid to acknowledge. The child is also your instinctive self, the self that still believes in fairytales and knows intuitively that the universe contains much that the father can neither deny nor explain away. The Erl-King is your 'higher' self or your soul self, that which is perfectly attuned to the entirety of cosmic consciousness in all its manifestations. The Erl-King is also the wild, primal man in you, the part of yourself that lives wild and free upon this planet, one and the same with the forces of nature and Life that govern our Earth. Do not suppose for a moment that your higher, soul self and your primal Earth self are somehow at opposite ends of the scale. In their purest forms each is an integral part of the other and together they represent the true beauty and God-liness that is man — you!

The story of the Erl-King is a sad one, most of all sad because it is so often true. How many men today try frantically to deny the existence of their 'wild' selves, the figure of the Horned God who walks within them all? And of those who seek to know the soul self, how many strive most earnestly to deny the forces of Nature and Life within? To achieve a denial of the polarities around which the Universal Energies spin and dance? The child within, the instinctive self, knows and understands well the nature of Spirit and how it manifests in many, many forms to make up the realm of Magic, Myth and Mystery. If the child is denied and silenced for long enough and hard enough then he dies, and with him dies all hope of ever knowing the Wild man, the Erl-King, the God-self within, for he can never be approached by the rational 'father' self.

Listen to your child-self, become attuned to your instinct; it is *not* violent, it is *not* angry, *it is aware*! Explore the realms of Fantasy and Magic to which the child will lead you (it *always* questions). Confront your fears and the manifestations of your 'dark' self; embrace the Erl-King and make him your own; his presence, in many ways, represents the limitations that you unconsciously cling to out of fear of fear itself. Let your walk through life lead you along the pathways of *all* the worlds, as you explore all the dimensions of your self (selves).

Throughout this book you will find each 'working' incorporating a story, a kind of a Legend. These are to be read and understood, insofar as they not only represent you (in *all* their characters) but the realms of Nature that it is fitting to worship and attune to. Most importantly the Legends awaken within the rational minds of men the child or Wild self and, as such, you will find yourself understanding not only women but the entirety of the Dual Principle that represents the Goddess and God of the Priesthood of Witchcraft.

The many forms of personal invocation will open for you the Faces of God and these Faces will integrate, through recognition, with your own. Jung considered these Faces as archetypes and this is true, but they are more than this, they are the Inheritance of Western man; they dwell in his racial memory; they exist in nature as separate energies that can be tapped and integrated with the self.

The Wiccan Priest, whilst adoring the Goddess and working Her Rites with the Priestesses of the Art at Full Moon, Dark Moon and New Moon respectively, may find, when working Solitary, the need to tap into the Full Moon Ritual only, of the female Rites, until such time as he is 'working' with a Priestess. The greater the knowledge you have of these Rituals the more chance you will have, upon finding a woman with whom to work, of showing her the Goddess within her own spirit.

So, herein lie the Wiccan Solar/Earth Rituals that will begin your Quest, the main dual aims of aligning yourself to the workings of a male Witch, and of aligning you with the Goddess through acknowledgement of Her God, King and Consort.

The Faces of God —
Visualisations and Invocations

We will begin by breaking into segments the different pantheons associated with Western Magick; the Gods and Goddesses that Witches find both familiar and comfortable, to allow you to progress with your own research in your own time, as this book is meant mainly for practical training and it is preferable that you follow through on theory as life allows. You will find it beneficial to seek out the myths and legends of Greek, Roman or Norse traditions, the Finno-Ugaric traditions, the Egyptian, Babylonian, Sumerian and Hebrew forms of worship and Magic, those of both North and South America, the Aboriginal legends of the Dreamtime and other shamanic traditions; have a major look at Qabbalism (see Recommended Reading List, p.183); you may lean towards the Gnostic or Rosicrucian paths; even the esoteric Christian traditions have many things in common with ancient and modern Paganism, as long as one avoids the fundamental denial of the Feminine Principle and the overshadowing 'fear' syndrome of control where self-worth is concerned. They will all show you that there is little or nothing new, and if you seek deeply enough you will most certainly find that the core of them all is identical; there is also much of interest in the early Eastern traditions, especially Tantra.

We will be attempting to meet the needs of our own inherant traditions of Celtic Britain, as, even though our blood is distributed throughout the world, it is still a very ancient blood that aligns us with our native inheritance and is *understood* through alliance with our geographic locations and the colourings of our traditions, through connecting with our environment and that environment's indigenous peoples: this tends to form a great tapestry of world understanding that needs to be seen through the wider vision and not the simple glance.

14

The traditions of our Celtic forbears, mingled with Western Magic in general, allows us to honour and acknowledge not only our past histories as fruitful in their own right, but our own present cultural and religious traditions that are available to us by the very nature of Palingenesis (blood and spirit in constant transubstantiation with the Cosmos).

No matter where in the world you may live many, many of us share a common religious origin that pre-dates the onset of Christianity by thousands of years; the Earth's people are really extremely tribal, still, despite advancing technological oneness, and our ideas of unification are to accept the tribes of others through honouring our own (as was aptly put to me many years ago by a very wise young man, 'a dog can be born in a stable, that doesn't make it a horse!'). We can love and honour the lands in which we live and we have our own unique tribal lineage to integrate with those lands, but we must not assume higher authority than those who are native to those lands; we must seek only to share what we are and what we know, which is, in many cases, especially in those of us of British or European descent, Celtic — aligning with our origins, our blood, is like a line of least resistance, that opens inner doorways by its very acceptance.

We are merging certain of the Gods of Ireland, Wales and Britain. Each of these aspects has its own legends and myths which, again, you would do well to follow up in your own time; this is not necessary to our purpose here. We have chosen twelve Faces of God for you to come to know through Invocation. Each of these Faces represents but one facet of your God and, therefore, of His Priests (we have attempted, for those of you studying or who are attuned to systems of Qabbalah, to align most of these Faces with the Sephiroth of the Tree of Life, described later).

The Rites

In the commonly accepted practices of Witchcraft the worship of Duality is shown as a Goddess and a God — this is to be acknowledged and accepted.

We are Witches of the Celtic tradition — if you are working at variance to your Palingenetic harmony you may find that profound confusion is the outcome; therefore, when you work with the Gods and Forces of your chosen Path do not diversify. Work with true line, in the tradition of your ancestors (lines *will* cross) and the form will become as it should be both today and tomorrow, for although we may draw sustenance, knowledge and vision from within the 'past' we do not work anywhere in time at all except *now* (which includes the Four Worlds of Annwn, Abred, Gwynvyd, Ceugant).

First, come to understand with your mind the deeper significance of each male Face, and then come to understand by using your heart which singular aspect of these Faces is aligned with your own higher desires, spirit, aspirations and, of course, your personality.

Second, work at invoking that Face as your 'mentor', as this Face will become your Inner Plane benefactor and will seek to manifest Himself through you and, because this Face is initially most comfortable for you, will become, again, your line of least resistance.

Thirdly you will, as Priest with his own archetypal connection, begin to work with the other Faces; no-one and nothing living (i.e. that which has a link with the Lifeforce itself) is one-dimensional or lacking in paradox, but is as multi-faceted as a jewel and hence as beautiful.

You must work at invoking these Faces (Forces) *singularly* to fully understand what they mean to you personally, as opposed to generally. You will be given the various aspects of each

16

Godform and you must work at refining, through visualisation, inspiration and invocation, your own true Priesthood by allowing each one of these Faces of God to touch your soul, possess your heart and guide your life. Only when this has been achieved will it be possible to perform the Rituals of your God as the Priestesses of the Moon perform the Rites of the Goddess.

You will work the Rituals of Esbat (Full Moon), Solstice and Equinox alone, if you have to. Again, as in *The Way of the Goddess*, we adjure you wherever possible to find a well-respected coven in which to train through Initiation and progression, as there is nothing to compare with a well-trained group of like-minded individuals all dedicated to the same path as you, performing the Rituals of your Art in unity of man/woman, Priest/Priestess, Goddess/God. If working within a coven structure, your High Priestess or High Priest will assist you and work with you when needed; but your invocation with personal Deity integration is to be done as a separate act of training, not when you gather together, as this is your road to Wholeness through personal dedication and power.

The Summonings

In each of the following examples you are to prepare yourself as if for normal Ritual:

1. Bathe with intent of purification.
2. Set up your Circle with the desired Ritual Tools: Altar; Candles (five), one for your Altar and the other four for the Elemental points at the outer edge of your Circle; Cup (Water); Wand (Fire); Athame (Air); Pentacle (Earth); Salt and Water in their own separate containers for consecration of your Circle; Wine; Robe (if you wear one).
3. Having read over the attributes of each Face of God and the Face that you have chosen to work with specifically, you are to cast your Circle, invoke the Elemental Guardians, go into meditation to level yourself out (four-fold breathing or a soft humming-chant will suffice), then consecrate the Salt and Water and seal the Circle with it, consecrate the Wine with Cup and Athame, and raise the Cup in honour of the Goddess and God and drink of it.
4. Sit or kneel (or stand, if preferable) where you will be comfortable for a span of time, and prepare your mind for the visualisation and invocation of the Face of God that you have chosen to work with on this night.

The many faces of the Solar/Earth God
* LLUGH * (pronounced hloo)
What He represents and how He appears

More of Light than the Sun — He is Lord of the Shining Light; is more than, but equal to, Artu (Arthur) insofar as His nature is Truth, and as such He can also represent Excalibur (the Sacred Sword). He is Divine Justice, Supreme Will, the Light and the protector of the Light that is the Way of the Priesthood. He represents the Hand of the Great Goddess, as the Spear of Light to humanity, and as such He represents the projection of your highest aspirations into your lifestyle and the (unattached) outcomes; He is the representation of your Initiation more than you as an ordinary mortal.

As with most of the Gods of the Celtic tradition He represents the fullness of life (including both love and the betrayal of love) and the transition of life, death and rebirth. His symbols (when seen) are the Spear and the Eagle (Golden Eagle).

On the Inner Planes He is seen as a shining Warrior, a Light Being with the Eagle (His symbol of Death) on His arm or in repose nearby. He holds His Spear, point down, before Him.

It is rarely possible to see His face directly (unless it is His desire that you do) as it tends to be too bright for the mortal eye.

(Kether — Light : the opposite in the Underworld — never 'negative', rather like Pluto)

* ARTU * (pronounced artoo)
What He represents and how He appears

He is the true symbol of the Sun made manifest. He can be equated with *all* the sacrificed Gods. He is the Brother, Lover and Son of the Great Goddess; is represented in *all* the Legends of Avalon as symbolising the seasons of Earth, Spirit and Man consecutively — He is the hope of the people for Knowledge and manifest Justice, as well as equality through unselfish love. He is one aspect of the Stag-King, Warrior of the people, whoever they may be, when oppression and hopelessness are the games played upon them.

He is the Great King, the Lord of Life and Death, the Initiated (anointed) One. His symbols are the Crown and the Dragon, and ofttimes also the Bear and the Stag (in fact all of these Sacred Animals are appropriate here).

He is seen on the Inner Planes dressed in crimson and is

crowned with a simple tri-pronged circlet of Gold, with shapes of Serpent or Dragon entwined within it (Ouroborous) representing the Wisdom of Cyclic Change. His symbols of duality are tattooed onto the cheeks of His face — on the left cheek is the tattoo of a Crow and on the right cheek is the tattoo of a Dragon. He carries a Sword of Light, point down, and is the bearer of the Light.

He *is* the Anointed One — Man, King and God as One. He is the symbol of Ascending Spirit, waxing and waning with the seasons of Sun, Sky and Seed, but He cannot exist on the physical Plane except through the love and embodiment of His Solar Earth Priests.

As a sacrificed King He dwells in the Mists of the Holy Isle-Outside-of-Time (Gwynvyd) until He is invoked into manifestation.

(Tiphareth — Sun)

* BELI * (pronounced bell-I)
What He represents and how He appears
He is also the symbol of the Sun but has no true manifest form — He is the symbol of the energy of the Solar Force. As such, invocation and meditation of Him means meditation on the symbol of the Sun or Solar Wheel itself.

N.B. This aspect of the Solar Deity is one of the earliest known and recorded Forms, as such His ancient inheritance causes Him to be extremely 'concentrated' (such other names for this aspect of Deity are: Bel, Baal, El, and he can be connoted with Ra — many of the authorities reason that this Face of God has travelled from the Middle East, across Europe to Britain, along with many other forms of God/esses that have been absorbed by our culture; in all or most cases the form of the name seems to indicate the term 'Lord').

* HU * (pronounced hyoo)
What He represents and how He appears
He is the God of the Grain — the Harvest Lord — the

God of Life, Inspiration, Growth, the Seed. As such He is also the bearer of the Seeds of Tomorrow.

He is Hu Gadarn, for your studies; He is Consort to the Earth Mother and is symbolic of the Rites of Passage associated with the Solar Wheel, especially the Solstices and Equinoxes. He is a God of fecundity, of joy, of giving and the sharing of the Earth's treasures.

He appears on the Inner Planes in green, with a red cloak and a many-pronged Crown of Gold — His hair is the colour of ripe grain. He is joyous, laughing. He is the epitome of fertility, both of thought and deed.

We feel very strongly, through encounter with Him, that the quote by Lewis Spence in *Magic Arts in Celtic Britain* (p.138) is extremely apt: 'Hu Gadarn was the Commander of the elements and the inhabitant of the Sun'.

N.B. He can be equated with the Greek form of Bacchus and also, due to his cyclic associations with the seasons, with Osiris.

(Netzach — Venus)

* LANCELET * (pronounced lanselet)
What He represents and how He appears

He, too, can be equated with Venus (as Hu, above), but more so with Mars due to His conflicts and powerful passions.

He is the symbol of the Seeker who has not yet found his way to the Grail. He also symbolises the One who sacrifices 'acceptable' existence for a greater cause. He is torn between His desire to fight for that greater cause (therefore the need for a dominant Artu-self) and His desire for personal love — this greater cause is the Grail herself (or one-ness with the Wellspring).

The invocation of Lancelet does not in any way reflect that you will be denied physical/personal love, but that you will sacrifice 'normal', accepted masculine practice and, unlike the non-Initiated man, you will view physical loving and the sexual act itself as an act of 'sacrifice' to be shared and given to the Goddess in woman — He therefore takes from the sex act the role of rutting or fornication and transforms it into a *divine act of love*. He does not do this only by way of sex, but by way of Love where His planet is concerned!

He is not the 'thinking' philosopher but the 'doing' philosophy.

He appears dressed in the deep red/orange of Sunset and bears a Cup (Grail?) in His left hand, as He faces you (symbolic of the fact that although He is most definitely a Warrior God His motives are passive, passionate and defensive, rather than active, analytical and confrontive), and there is always wonder in His eyes.

N.B. He can be equated with the Titan, Prometheus, whose motives in manifesting Fire for humanity were continually threatened by the 'soul' of the other Gods (change again symbolised by the Eagle in this story), and whose only surcease was the Night (the Feminine, also the Grail) and His passionate purpose for continued sacrifice, i.e. Love and the belief in the 'rightness' of His reason.

(Geburah — Mars)

* MERLYN * (the Younger and the Elder; both considered separate for your purposes)
What He represents and how He appears

He has two Faces. You are to invoke Him with that awareness as He may choose to appear with either the younger or the older Face.

He is the God of Learning; Master of Magic, Mystery, Movement; of that which is both ancient and intelligent; of story and legend he is famed; the true Bard — there is not one amongst us who has not yearned to know Him and to know what He knows, for He is the epitome of arcane, Magical, Masculine Wisdom (of the Sea, He is also the counterface of the great and legendary Morgan-le-Fey).

He is, firstly, the Messenger of the other Faces of the Master;

of those who dwell in Caer Ceugant, and is also the Messenger of the Goddess and the Herald of the Future. Do not seek Him as His ancient self only, as He can be as bright and shining as either Llugh or Artu, but after another fashion. He also represents the law-bringer but He is not a Warrior God. He carries a (*the*) Book and a (*the*) Harp; the Book symbolises Knowledge and Truth through experience, and the Harp is the Music of Life and the purveyor of Enchantment.

He is invoked in either His aspect of Master of Magic or His aspect of Truthsayer, Enchanter and Prophet; in either of these aspects He may appear either young or old.

The Face of Merlyn the Younger, on the Inner Planes, is cowled and robed in a cloak the colour of mist or early morning light. The Book will be in His right hand and the Harp in His left (He may even let you look into the Book!).

As Merlyn the Elder he also represents Time, in which case He will be cowled and robed in black and will carry a Scythe in His left hand and the Book in His right. When invoking this Master of Magic you must remember that He has an Achilles' Heel (as does everyone), and it is this: He will be swayed by His dogmatic belief in the Law to the point where He will not bend and, as Time's natural path is *change*, He is undone by Nimue who represents Tomorrow.

N.B. There is no figure in any other pantheon that is quite like Merlyn, or as profound in impact (except, perhaps, for figures such as Chronos, Charon, Hermes).

(Merlyn the Younger: Hod-Mercury
Merlyn the Elder: Binah-Saturn)

* CERNUNNOS * (pronounced Kernoonos) also known as Cerne, Herne.

What He represents and how He appears

Here is our Great Lord of the Untamed! He is the Green-Man, even Robin Hood! The Wild Magic of woods, forests, mountain, deep valley and animal (including the animal-self). He is the Primal in you and as such He has been greatly feared in 'civilised' consciousness (early Christians, and even today's, have turned Him around so as to appear evil, which He most definitely is not).

Women yearn for Him in their dreams (and even in their waking states if they fear not their own wildness). He is raw force.

In His Earth-Plane nature He is invoked at risk; 'Why?' you may ask. Why? Because most men have succeeded in burying His Face and His essence within the very depths of their unconscious selves out of fear (the fear that sexuality is somehow evil), and unless they have done the work with the Shadow in their own natures they will be shocked by Him (Oh, what a shame! cry all the Priestesses of Wicca).

Therefore, be aware of risk when you invoke Him and plead a little that He work *slowly* into your consciousness as we are quite certain that He can be responsible for all manner of rape and other unacceptable sexual reactions to His millenia-long repression!

He is like the Greek Nemesis insofar as He is invoked, through Ritual, in matters pertinent to the Wild Places when it is necessary to prevent destruction of his natural domain — and this is to assist Him and the Great Earth-Mother in their battle to preserve our Galactic Inheritance from those who would rob Her blind!

He is invoked when you need longevity required in the Great Rite, and He is also invoked to protect His Priests and Priestesses from danger directly associated with their beliefs. However, invoke Him you must, as part of your training, but you must *earth* Him when you are done, as you will be taught (see page 62).

He is the personification of the Four Elements and when invoked He will appear as an enormous, physically powerful Man/God — vines and leaves will be His mantle and the Horns of the Great Stag grow from His forehead. He is both beautiful and awe-ful and He will impart that proud, free, wild energy to you.

He is the epitome of the majestic King of the Forests!

N.B. He can be equated with Pan of the Greek pantheon. (Malkuth — Earth; also Da'ath — when considering His energy)

* GWYDION * (pronounced gooidion)
What He represents and how He appears
He is the inheritance of Math, Lord of the Underworld, to mankind. He is a Master of Vision and as such is the Inner Plane teacher to the Priest of Witchcraft.

He is invoked to develop personal power and the dignity without affectation that is the hallmark of a well-trained Priest. It is the *quality* of your attitude — you are not prim, or conservative, or completely tame. When you invoke Him you invoke the Inner Teachings relative to the Sight.

He is associated with two of the greater Faces of the Goddess in the Celtic pantheon — Rhiannon and Arianhrod (the latter, who was His 'sister', He also co-joined with to produce the awe-inspiring Force of Llugh).

He is seen, on the Inner Planes, dressed in leather and furs with a cloak about His shoulders the colours of which comprise russet (Autumn) and the deep, rich colours of violets; you can almost smell His rich, loamy presence. Joining the cloak at the neck is the Equal-Armed Cross (the Four Elements) to show that He is Master of the Principles of Earth.

He bears a sword which he keeps in a silver scabbard, symbolic of the fact that He and the Goddess are a unity; that He is Her ally; that They are 'as the Athame to the Cup'.

He wears a headdress of Crow Feathers upon His head like a crown, and he stands very straight — He is not cocky, He is proud; not vain, but dignified.

Nothing attacks Him — He is representative of the Authority of your Path and has the emanations of Llugh and Artu within Him.

(Chesed — Jupiter)

* MANANNAN * (pronounced manannan)
What He represents and how He appears

God of the Sea; He is, as such, God of the sub-conscious mind. He is approached when you have irrational fears or unresolved problems. He is one's primordial beginnings and represents all that dwells beneath the surface of the supposed civilised veneer of man.

He is also the essence of the Shapechanger and imparts the gift of invisibility — to be seen, but not seen. He bestows the ability to 'see' that which cannot be seen, and as such He is also associated with scrying in all its aspects and the Astral Plane (Gwynvyd).

He represents protection associated with your ability to delve deeply beneath the surface of your rational mind.

He appears as a nebulous, mist-moving, not-quite-there God of the Sea. He appears differently each time He is invoked, but the tinge of green about Him and the unmistakable smell of brine will accompany Him at each working.

It is wise to invoke His aid when preparing for any form of initiation as He will assist you to 'sneak up' on those fears and phantasms that inhabit your subconscious self, and which can block the heights (or depths) that you will seek as part of your Path.

He is the essence of Changeability.

N.B. He can be equated with Neptune.

(Yesod — Moon)

* DIANCECHT * (pronounced dian-ket)
What He represents and how He appears

He is the Celtic God of Healing. He is associated with Wells, the Cauldron of Cerridwen, and His symbols are both the Mortar and the Pestle.

There is no set description of Him, but He is invoked in all matters pertaining to Healing. He is the God of the Herb and the natural healing agents that come to us from the wild, as well as being the representative of Universal Healing. He will, however, usually appear in a forest grove (a nemeton) with a Fire and a Cauldron, surrounded with the Wildcrafted herbs of His Art.

N.B. We can associate Him with Apollo (in one of the aspects) but have not given Him a Qabbalistic or Planetary association.

* TALIESIN * (pronounced tal-i-essin)
What He represents and how He appears

'I have been in many shapes before I attained a congenial form. I have been a narrow blade of a sword; I have been a drop in the air; I have been a shining star; I have been a word in a book; I have been a book in the beginning; I have been a light in a lantern a year and a half; I have been a bridge for passing over threescore rivers; I have journeyed as an eagle; I have been a boat on the sea; I have been a director in battle; I have been a sword in the hand; I have been a shield in fight; I have been a string of a harp; I have been enchanted for a year in the foam of water. There is nothing in which I have not been.' (from *The Book of Taliesin*)

He is the God of 'projected Knowledge' — He is, literally, the force behind the spoken word. Whilst keeping alive within our Palingenetic memory the instinctive knowledge that has been inherited from the past through discipline and seeking, He also projects that knowledge into the future — therefore He could also, today, be considered as the wisdom behind technology (as opposed to technology itself).

He is as shamanic as the other Faces of God insofar as He represents the essence of them all, along with the curious ability to transform inspiration into actuality; thus He is the very heart of Alchemy.

He can be seen, when invoked, surrounded with a glowing ovoid of faintly blue Light. He stands before an Altar upon which rest all the Ritual Tools that lay upon your own. He is neither inside nor outside as He dwells upon the border of all things; the only exception to your own Ritual Tools is a Feather pen, which symbolises the spoken word made manifest (there is, however, no Book, as He also represents the disciplined racial and intellectual memory).

He always stands upon the Threshold between today and tomorrow, thus we have found it easiest to invoke Him at the hours between Sunset and Night.

N.B. He can be equated with Uranus of the Greek pantheon. (Chokmah — sphere of the Zodiac)

* MATH * (pronounced math)
What He represents and how He appears

He is the God of the Underworld — the benevolent, just and beneficent Ruler of the Between-World (Annwn). Lewis Spence says of Him, in *Magic Arts in Celtic Britain* (p.32), 'Math was able to hear without difficulty "every sound of speech that reached the air", he was utterly righteous and just in his dealings with gods and men, and was the great diviner, teacher and master of omens.'

He has been equated with Manawyddan and Pryderi, also of the British Gods, and has none of the connotations associated with other Gods of the Underworld; i.e. He is rather beautiful, albeit dark and deep, and His methods of training are to enlighten rather than to judge. Absolutely all the Gods (and most of the Goddesses) of the British pantheon are Threshold Dwellers and Math is no exception — Math is invoked at times of transition; the end of one cycle and the beginning of the other is where He resides, as we of Magic do not consider life and death as being purely physical functions, or as absolutes, but pertinent to any change that has that appearance (e.g. Initiation in all its forms, either through the Will or at the hands of the Gods).

He appears, bidden or unbidden, at times of transition — to assist in the rebirth so to speak. He is cloaked in a mantle of Crow Feathers, from head to foot; His hair and eyes are as dark as the Bird He represents. He is also a Shapechanger and as such He may not appear as entirely human, but Bird-like or even just the Bird itself. Despite His being a God of the Underworld He is especially invoked at, or just prior to, Dawn — you will hear His voice in the first birdsong of the day and the interpreting of omens is by way of what they say and/or the direction and 'shape' of their flight.

At times He can be seen lying down with His feet in the lap of a Maiden.

N.B. He can be equated with Pluto, in some respects, of the Greek pantheon.

(Da'ath — Chiron)

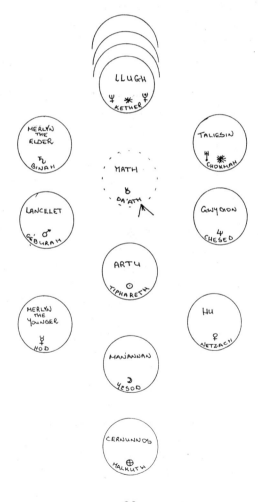

The Rites of the Priest of the Sun

The Rites of the Priest of the Sun are done daily. The most auspicious times of the Solar Day to work are at Sunrise, Midday, Sunset; these are times of transition (similar to the triple cycle of the Moon). They are not necessarily times of Ritual, more of opening up your awareness to the forces of the waxing and waning of the Day. The process of awareness is such that you will be breaking down the usual time barriers that a normal daily routine ensures you have. The process of setting the alarm, getting up, showering, breaking the night's fast, going about the daily round of necessity that is required of you will be forever broken by altering the treatment of the routines that surround any mortal.

Some of us will automatically get up at Sunrise, light a simple stick of incense, a candle, and form a focus within the mind of completion — acknowledging that all that has gone before this day is gone! that with the coming of the Dawn is a new reality that is affected by our interplay within its revolution; it is important not to become complacent with your life — to view it from continually 'innocent' eyes and to accept it as 'born'.

A simple invocation will suffice, mainly as acknowledgement of the God with whom you are allied:

I summon the force of the Light of the World!
Blessed be the King, powers of the mighty Seed!

If your day were to permit, it is always a good time then to go back to bed, even for just an hour, and to try to sleep. The dreams that come to you after intentioned waking can be of importance to your Magic; write them down, they can be among the most intense that you will experience.

The experience of linking with the full tide of the Solar Day is to acknowledge the power of the might of the Lord of Life, in

His prime (both within yourself and within the domain of the Earthplane). To set aside five minutes at noontide is to allow the forces to again pervade your spirit without expectation. Get away from workmates for those five minutes and either meditate silently or walk in whatever natural setting you can find.

A simple invocation would be:

I summon for me the Master of Magic!
Lord of the Powers of Flight!

The third aspect of the Solar Day, Sunset, is to be treated as your descent into the Underworld of the Day (the womb of the Night is the time of the Goddess), it is the secret tide, the time to switch off from all problems, to reassess what has occurred for you during the passed Solar Day, and for many in Magic it is the time for play or work, depending on how much needs to be accomplished within your Path. All workings that occur in the night are based on Planetary hours.

Again, keep the invocation at Sunset relatively simple:

Eagle of Gold descends to the Deep,
I invoke the Wild Magic, gifts of Silence!

The Summoning

To summon one or other of the Faces of God is to call upon that Force as an external agent and not as an archetype. To summon is to request communication and integration through interaction without preconceived expectation of what the particular Force fully represents.

Until such time as a substantial Inner Plane contact has been made you may be working hard without satisfaction — you can only ever learn so much from books and the opinions of others, and the truth of your Magic will come through personal experience and communication with those beyond the Veil.

They need to be summoned through the knowledge of (a) what it is that you wish to know, and (b) your prior knowledge of what it is that you summon. You will need to ensure caution insofar as the Force that you summon *must* align, in concept and philosophy, with what you know; you must be prepared, through correct cleansing and protection, through focus within a well-prepared Ritual Circle, to ensure that you do not pick up stray energies, as these type of workings are like iron filings to a magnet!

To honour the Force that you summon you must be prepared to keep adequate records of the encounter; you must seek knowledge and not self-gain; you must be prepared to follow through on the things that you learn and not just activate the Forces for the sake of curiosity or experimentation.

Therefore, you would summon the Faces for their *properties* as follows:

Llugh For the attunement and refinement of your own sense of personal power. In matters relevant to Justice, Will, Aspiration. *Artu* In matters relevant to hope, equilibrium, education, government, religion.

Beli In matters relevant to honour; to come to know the true self; practical, personal achievement

Hu To assist you in the processes of growth of any project that takes time for completion; can assist in directing your Path along lines of natural growth.

Lancelet In matters relevant to love; questing; environmental change that is personally oriented; in battle (whatever the battle may be).

Merlyn The Advisor — He will advise you in matters occult and philosophic; the seeking of future knowledge that may have its matrix in the past; He is a Truthsayer.

Cernunnos To advise you in all matters of Earth, of freedom, of sexuality. He is summoned in times of 'attack'; to come to know your deeper Wild side.

Gwydion To aid your ability to 'see'; personal dissection of emotional interference caused by conditioning; again for the inspirations of Magic; for illumination on any subject.

Manannan To see beneath the surface of things; to recognise deceit and illusion in any situation (or in yourself); His Force taps into the collective unconscious; in all matters where you need protection or a cloak of invisibility.

Diancecht In matters pertaining to health — of the self, others, and/or the environment.

Taliesin Representing the Force of the spoken or the written word; the Force of Discipline; for any moves that are to take place; to assist the memory; in learning; in all matters of transmutation.

Math He can be considered the masculine counterpart of the High Priestess card in the Tarot; is so strongly similar to Pluto that you will learn just about anything at His hands that He wishes to teach you — as He is an Underworld Force He will choose the teaching that He wishes to impart without your conscious connection. He teaches through trance, vision, dreams. He is also your Judge!

Part Two:
Earthdawn

From out of the depths of the Oceans of the Self comes an inherent desire to seek after immortality.

We have grown in mind and spirit, past the point of unreserved faith, to seek that immortality through understanding not only our possible origins but also our possible total destiny. Not only do we seek as individuals but we have come full circle to realise the dynamics of a quantum whole. The seeker after personal identity through reincarnation and genetic/environmental inheritance, and trying to evaluate who and what we are by way of 'humanising' spirit and energy, has led to the recognition of our supreme mortality. Those of us who cannot help but to seek through science for a medium of spirit will find it in the realms of possibilities raised in quantum physics — seeing, through an electron microscope, infinity at work; universes being born and dying, galaxies of suns and centres, all mirroring the external space in which our planet, and hence our physical bodies, dwell. The ancients had it right all along!

Only by following through consciously on an understanding of the disintegrate self can we see the patterns of a greater whole of which we are an integral part. This understanding is so shamanic, as it inevitably leads to understanding that it is our present actions only that matter to the evolving whole, and that the imprint of following lines of least resistance, magically as well as personally and spiritually, can only result in that which is important to our survival, again both cosmically and personally — scary stuff!

I had a man who was dying of cancer ask me at one of my workshops to tell him about death and that which follows. He hated my answer! I told him that I would tell him after I got there. He considered that to be opting out of my responsibility as a teacher of things occult and spiritual. It would have been extremely presumptuous of me to attempt to lift a veil that can only be lifted through personal experience of an event. We perceive personal views of death and the later experience of it to be the Inner Sanctum of the Holy of Holies; one can never fully understand an experience until it is personally felt — each person has their own personal views, and speaking from desire does not necessarily have anything to do with the truth. The personality taps into the greater whole and 'knows' all about transition — the personality is the spirit's interpretation, in linear ways, of the 'seen' universe and is its outward expression, in comprehensible terms, of that which cannot be comprehended by the conscious mind.

The exercises in this section deal with transition, from one way of emoting and practising life to another. Isn't that life? Isn't it death?

So all that we can do is to explore with what we know to be valid at this moment in time — bear in mind that it will change with time and from person to person; this is a natural law and one of the first that you must know, one that none of us can afford to forget or else the ego will take over from what is truth, just so that we can show others what we think we know — 'Good boy, don't I impress with what I say!' — careful, careful!

There seems to be rife misunderstanding in many areas of the occult which states that Witchcraft and Magic are somehow disconnected — let me assure you that they are synonymous, and to have true balance one needs to be able to work magic within the natural world as well as in the worlds of mind and spirit.

Therefore, the seeking after immortality is the integration of the individual within the greater patterns of Earth, Moon, Sun and Star through personalised understanding.

In this chapter we will be looking at the nature of the number 4 pertinent to the Earth — the Elements, the major Ritual Tools, the Four Worlds of the Celtic Occultist, the Circles of Light and Dark and how they are 'worked' — and we will seek to integrate them all so that you can set up your Circle, call forth the Guardians of the Threshold, consecrate your Ritual Tools and Walk the Paths of the Four Worlds.

Firstly we will give you a breakdown of what will be covered in total. Study these until they are familiar.

There is an Elemental Legend inclusive within each Ritual working that you are to 'walk' within, through creative visualisation; each one of them is to be dealt with in two ways:

1. Each Legend is meant to act as a puzzle — there are Keys within each one that will strike symbolically at the chords of the mind for understanding *your* part within the Elements.

2. Each Legend is designed to evoke an emotion so that you will not just intellectualise the exercise; without the force of focus engendered by mind and heart combined, your work will have no impact whatsoever.

It is necessary to remember that each character, place and situation are all facets of yourself, they are internal as well as environmental.

The final part of this section will deal, specifically, with ethics: the influence of thoughts, emotions and actions on the astral as well as the greater Evolving Whole.

The Elements

We will be giving both common and Celtic considerations to each Element as well as an understanding of their environmental implications. Included in this chapter is the exercise known as the Book of Elements, which is your way of breaking down the parts of yourself into recognisable quarters for the purpose of self-awareness; this book is meant to aid you in an understanding of how socio/cultural and religious conditioning has influenced you away from a natural flow. I believe that understanding through the use of Elemental Invocation is absolutely necessary, for without it the whole physical dimension, or dimension of life, is unbalanced (which is probably what is wrong with the world today!).

The Threshold of Gorias
The Element of AIR
The invoking direction of this threshold is to the East; this represents the *Place of the Rising Sun*, and is therefore said to be the birthplace of the Gods; the Sword dwells here, the symbol of a greater Will than mere earthly desires; the determination to transcend present limitations; it is equated with inspiration that comes from seemingly nowhere and is the intuitional self that sees beyond the rational. It represents, essentially, intelligence — not the capacity to learn but rather the ability to understand that which is learned.

This dimension is understood by the axiom 'To Will', and in your Circle it is shown as Incense, Sword, Athame.

The time of the Solar Day is Sunrise; the time of the Solar Year is Spring Equinox.

The colour associated with Air is yellow or white; its gender is masculine/feminine; its Elemental is the Sylph; environmentally it is wind, the atmospheric sky, the air we breathe; within the self it is the air we breathe and the oxygen within our bodies that sustains life.

The Zodiacal applications are Gemini, Libra, Aquarius; the Qabbalistic Archangelic Force is Raphael; the Elemental King is Paralda; its Hermetic symbol is:

the invoking Pentagram used to open the Threshold is:

Its Mythos accepts the 'Unity of the Sun King with the Daughter of the Moon — His Initiation as Priest/King.'

The Threshold of Finias
The Element of FIRE
The invoking direction of this Element in the southern hemisphere is North, in the northern hemisphere it is South; this represents the *Sun at His zenith*; the Staff dwells here as it is the Communicator and is, therefore, all modes of outward expression; one *must* be understood — in our world people tend to twist the truth to suit their needs, and it is paramount that the Priest seeking Caer Ceugant should first and foremost seek the honesty that will enable him to sift the illusions from the truth, as the mind will certainly play fantasy games with the gullible and it is easy to get caught up in these illusions to your own detriment, and ultimately the ripples of folly affect the Evolving Whole. Actual 'touchings' occur when the Circle is cast and the Gods are invoked, so be a little wary.

This dimension is understood by the axiom 'To Dare', and in your Circle it is shown as Candle, Brazier, Wand, Staff.

The time of the Solar Day is Midday; the time of the Solar Year is Summer Solstice.

The colour associated with Fire is red; its gender is masculine; its Elemental is the Salamander; environmentally it is all forms of fire, from hearth to bushfire, from lightning and electricity to solar and nuclear fission; within the self it is our body's natural warmth that sustains life, right down to the atomic energy in transition.

Its Zodiacal applications are Aries, Leo, Sagittarius; the Qabbalistic Archangelic Force is Michael; the Elemental King is Djinn; its Hermetic symbol is:

the Invoking Pentagram used to open the Threshold is:

Its Mythos accepts the 'Symbolic Sacrifice of the Sun King — Transformation of One Form into Another — Cyclic Change'. The Phoenix lives!

The Threshold of Murias
The Element of WATER
The invoking direction of this Element is West; this represents the *Place of the Setting Sun*, therefore ofttimes being called the realm of the dying Gods; the Grail dwells here, the symbol of the Cauldron of Cerridwen, the Womb of Life, the Place of Questing beyond the Veil. The Sun setting in this place is your concern here. The dark dwells beneath the surface of conscious thought. This is the place of the Island Remembered and the deaths of outmoded thought and deed, of integral importance to the Witch. It is the symbol of emotion and can be called the realm of sorrows, for here all our dreams lie waiting, fulfilment yet another day away. It is the Chalice and the Goddess and the part of yourself that is the most difficult to come to terms with — we can control many things but emotion tends to control us, even though it is our own. For men it is necessary to reach deeply into the Cauldron to tackle the 'monsters' that dwell therein.

This dimension is understood by the axiom 'To Keep

Silence', and in your Circle it is shown as the Cup; Water.

The time of the Solar Day is Sunset; the time of the Solar Year is the Autumn Equinox.

The colour associated with Water is deep blue; its gender is feminine; its Elemental is the Undine; environmentally it is ocean, rain, river, ice, snow, dew, all underground water, lakes, pools, inland seas and all waters that sustain planetary life — all ruled by the Moon; within the self it is the liquid that forms the waters of the body.

Its Zodiacal applications are Cancer, Scorpio, Pisces; its Qabbalistic Archangelic Force is Gabriel; the Elemental King is Nixsa; its Hermetic symbol is:

the invoking Pentagram used to open the Threshold is:

Its Mythos accepts the 'Descent through the Underworld, Power from the Dark Lord (the personal Pluto) to the Maiden of Initiation.'

The Threshold of Falias
The Element of EARTH
The invoking direction of this threshold in the southern hemisphere is South, in the northern hemisphere it is North; this represents the *Place of Pre-birth*, hence re-birth in potential; the Shield dwells here, the symbol of protection and summoning, the doorway between the worlds; our ability to exist in the mortal world is invoked here — practicality, determination, the preservation of physical life, including our own bodies and the respect of the body, the ability to cement ideas, inspirations, etc., can only be achieved with a strong foundation; this realm represents knowledge, both practical and philosophical/arcane.

This dimension is understood by the axiom 'To Know', and

in your Circle is shown by the Pentacle, Shield, Drum.

The time of the Solar Day is Midnight; the time of the Solar Year is the Winter Solstice.

The colour associated with Earth is deep green; its gender is feminine/masculine; its Elemental is the Gnome; environmentally it is earth, stones, sand, mineral and metal, the makeup of plant and animal life; within the self it is bone muscle, sinew, all solidity right down to the cellular level.

Its Zodiacal applications are Taurus, Capricorn, Virgo; its Qabbalistic Archangelic Force is Uriel; the Elemental King is Ghobb; its Hermetic symbol is:

the Invoking Pentagram used to access the Threshold is:

Its Mythos accepts the 'Rebirth of a Sun God, the Boyhood and Training of a King.'

The Four Worlds

Annwn (pronounced annoon)

The Underworld; the primal abyss; the place of pre-life; the unconscious wherein dwells all genetic memory, lost places, lost faces, unformed potential and the progression of all life. This is the place of the Dragon-Force, and the Dragon dwells at the mouth of the abyss and guards the untapped treasure reverently!

The House of Annwn is the 'Tail of the Dragon'.

We enter this place as our greatest test — time of grief, time of trial, the prospect of Initiation, to life as well as to the passage of the Priest. It is eternal night, darkness of Space, deepest of silences. At the very back of conscious thought we have all been there, or at least sensed that domain — at times we all see frighteningly into the void, but madness dwells there for the unwary and we all tread the extended bridge of Knowledge before seeking the treasure, which is purely the test of self against self.

Here, go all Legends known, goeth the Hero in search of the Kingdom — to seek and to conquer what we meet along the Path inwards.

'[This] divine interaction, we are told, began in the depths of Annwn, or the abyss, and life underwent a course of gradual change from the lowest forms, including reptilian and other shapes, to the highest spiritual conceptions. Annwn, indeed, appears as a still lower phase than Abred; if he has not led a "righteous" life, at the end of existence he may descend into Annwn once more doomed to experience a second period of upward growth.' (Lewis Spence *The Magic Arts in Celtic Britain*) He appears to mean the 'not-world'.

Abred (pronounced abreth)

The manifest Earthplane. The place where 'life' is acknowledged; is very strongly connected to the conscious mind, to action and reaction in life's path; as such, the Priest must be aware of the spaces he dwells within and the ripples that his life is bound to create, as free-choice has to be both claimed and owned and then responded to responsibly. The task of the Priest is to learn to tread softly in time.

The House of Abred is the 'Body of the Dragon'.

We all act out our own personal mythos through experience, and the recognition of not only what we are doing but how we are doing it is your concern here.

Abred is your physical temple, your sacred space in which you work magic; it is interwoven with Annwn, with Gwynvyd and thence with Ceugant, and if this is not forgotten it will make living a clearer experience.

Gwynvyd (pronounced gooinvyth)

The Inner Planes; the Places beyond the Veil; can be equated with the 'higher Astral' (unlike Annwn, the lower Astral where also demons dwell). Entry into this realm is through controlled magical imagery, controlled Pathwalking; the Arts and the inspiration that evokes art, poetry, music, dance and creative dreaming. Our higher selves dwell there, the knowledge of Annwn and Abred are clear there; the ramifications of our magic dwell there for all to see!

The path of the Evolving Whole is registered there and the Gods meet with us in whatever form They choose through the medium of Gwynvyd. It is also the realm of illusion that can trap the foolish by its glamour (meant in the older sense, of 'spell', which is why I place emphasis on the word 'control'.

The House of Gwynvyd is the 'Head of the Dragon'. Does it not then control Annwn and Abred? In essence it is opposing Annwn.

Ceugant (pronounced caigant)

Like Mount Olympus this is the dwelling place of the Gods. It relates to the non-conscious-accessible realm that is the oversoul of time, energy and space. It truly is the Great Wheel, the Spiral Dance, the dimension of total possibility. It cannot be understood by our minds (at this point in evolution, I might add) because no matter what we might understand, know, discover or consider possible, there will always be more.

The House of Ceugant is the 'Dragon's Breath', or the whole of the Dragon; which brings to mind the axiom 'The whole is always greater than the sum of its parts'.

Ceugant is continually expanding, therefore how can we ever hope to know it? There is pleasure in this thought! Mystery is, in its own right, power, and it is our inalienable right to seek that Mystery; any who have crossed the threshold of Gwynvyd, even once, will seek that Mystery.

Ceugant is the greatest gift to the Evolving Whole — we *never* go past the Universe's next trick!

Summary

The House of *Annwn* is the 'Tail of the Dragon'.
The House of *Abred* is the 'Body of the Dragon'.
The House of *Gwynvyd* is the 'Head of the Dragon'.
The House of *Ceugant* is the 'Breath of the Dragon'.

The Dragon is ourselves.

Keys of consideration

Annwn: refers to the Underworld; things not yet in form; the Unconscious; the primal abyss.

Abred: refers to the manifest Earthplane, the realms of physical existence; the physical bodies of all things; the conscious mind; manifestation.

Gwynvyd: refers to the realms of the Higher Astral, the Inner Planes; controlled magical imagery; the arts; inspiration.

Ceugant: refers to the non-(conscious)-accessible realms of the High Gods; the dimension of totality-in-continuum; the Universal Life-Force; our highest aspirations that are not bound by desire.

Ritual Tools

Consider, if you will, the axiom 'As above, so below'; we are not asking you to just go out and procure your Ritual Tools indiscriminately. Care, contemplation, inner perception and age-old shamanic 'attraction' are all to be considered in your Quest for the Sacred.

Symbolic in your Ritual Circle, representative of the Element of Air, Most Sacred of the Ancient 4, is the *Sword*.

Symbolic in your Ritual Circle, representative of the Element of Fire, Most Sacred of the Ancient 4, is the *Staff*.

Symbolic in your Ritual Circle, representative of the Element of Water, Most Sacred of the Ancient 4, is the *Grail*.

Symbolic in your Ritual Circle, representative of the Element of Earth, Most Sacred of the Ancient 4, is the *Shield*.

The Sword

The actual expression of the Most Sacred of the Ancient 4 is accumulated as follows: the black-hilted, double-edged dagger, known as *Athame*, has all the attributes of the Sword and is used by Witches worldwide as the extended Will.

In our tradition this Tool is, for the most part, hand-made. We have to date had no trouble finding a blacksmith or a knife-smith who is involved in similar practices who, for an unconditional price, will assist in forging this weapon (that never draws blood).

Although the traditional metal is iron, we know of those who have used steel, silver, bronze and stone, as well as mixed metals of significance; some will set their Blade with inlaid runes, some have long, tapering Blades, some are waving like a kris, some are sickled and three I know are mathematically proportionate to one of the Egyptian pyramids; some have cross-pieces artistically and personally designed, perhaps set with certain stones; the hilts I have seen defy limitation except in the mind of the Priest or Priestess; some are carved from ebony in the likeness of the body of Isis with hand-carven silver capital, some are willow spirals whilst others are bound in red-belly black snakeskin. They are rowan or oak, or velvet entwined in silken braid. All are unique and either hand-done or hand-finished.

Of course, if the Fates decree, you may actually come by a Sword — it is not necessary and should not replace the energy you have imbued into your Athame.

Your Athame, when procured, is taken into your Circle and consecrated. It is *never* left lying about. It is *never* used outside the domain of your Circle. It is *never* used to draw blood. It is a tool of pure Invocation, it represents your Priesthood, your Truth, your Will and your Power.

The Staff

The actual expression of the Most Sacred of the Ancient 4 representing the Staff is the Wand (some of us have a Staff also, this is personal preference). It is used in all acts of summoning and represents the Word (communication of intent) which is most important to know, as many Workings are not conducive to the spoken word and the Wand acts as your Inner Plane Merlyn, conducting communication into Caer Gwynvyd and deeper.

When it is cut for shaping, this Tool is measured from elbow to the tip of your middle finger. As this Tool is the Communicator it is also important to realise that you cannot cut a living branch for the purpose of making your Wand and/or Staff. I have a Staff of Elm-wood, the tree having been blown down in a violent thunderstorm (consequently it is imbued with the energy of the storm); and a Wand of Rowan twigs, taken from the dead branch of a living tree. My High Priest has a Wand of Oak, found cut down by the local council clean-up, and a Staff of knobby Eucalypt found in the forest near a most magical, wild and windswept beach.

The Wand can be left plain, oiled with linseed; it can be

painted, carved, hung with bells and feathers, set with runes of silver and gold, it can have a crystal as a capital, be hollowed out and filled with ground semi-precious stones or simply have your Ritual Name written in pen and ink down its length.

Your Wand, when made, is taken into your Circle and consecrated, then wrapped in cloth or leather. It is *never* left lying around. It is *never* used outside of the domain of a Ritual Circle. It is your Tool of Merlyn-Magic, your Creative Force, your deepest Voice.

The Grail

The actual expression of the Most Sacred of the Ancient 4 representing the Grail is the Cup (sometimes called the Chalice, sometimes known as the Cauldron). It is used to consecrate the wine, it is also used for the art of scrying, and as such it is also a Mirror.

The Cup is the Grail remembered, the Cornucopia, symbol of the fertilising power of the Waters of Life, also the Womb. It is the symbol, within your Circle, of the Goddess, and as such it represents Love and will be upon your Altar as a representative of the Priestess (if not in the flesh, most assuredly in spirit). It is the vessel of emotion, most necessary in all acts of Will-working.

It is mostly silver or silver-plate, as this is the metal of the Moon (as gold is the metal of the Sun), but can be turned of wood. I have seen two that were of beautiful Venetian glass (perhaps a little impractical if one moves around too frequently, as they do break). This Tool is as much a symbol of the Great Goddess as the Staff is the symbol of the God in his many Faces that you seek!

However hard you try it is most difficult to have a Cup made, and for this reason I suggest that you buy it — do not quibble over cost, though, if it is what you want.

The Shield

The actual expression of the Most Sacred of the Ancient 4 representing the Shield is the Pentacle (sometimes a Drum). It is used in all acts of Invocation, especially relating to the Elements, Elementals, Threshold Guardians. It literally represents the Earth. It is used specifically at all banishings, house blessings, consecrations, bindings and protections. Its summoning powers, when properly prepared, lend surcease to physical and material hindrance.

The most common and acceptable form of Pentacle is the copper disc; this is usually about 15 cm. in diameter and about ⅛ cm. in thickness. The disc is hand-carved with the Sigils of your Art, the main theme being the Pentagram. It is then buried in the path of the waxing Moon from New Moon to Full (during which time, all going well, it should be turning from red-brown to green, the colour of Venus), at which time it is dug up and consecrated in your Circle.

Alternatives to copper have been highly polished wood, clay, stone, parchment, wax, and one most beautiful piece sliced from the inside of a Thunder-egg complete with natural crystal centre!. I have not known of any other materials being used, as we feel that they would be contrary to the Element of Earth. One alternative (although best if you had the traditional Pentacle as well) is the Drum. Every Witch should have one. Whether it is the traditional tambour or one of the easily available shaman drums, they are exceptional Ritual Tools and can be practically used for the inner voyaging, as the sound is ridden like the horse that so many shamanic traditions named them after.

Like the Cup and the other Ritual Tools it is kept in the secret places of the Witch and not used outside of a Ritual Circle.

Setting Up a Ritual Circle

Wherever you are to work your Rituals is to be considered as a Temple, even before it is properly prepared as a work-space. The Key to preparation is *simple perfection*. You should eat nothing for about three hours prior to the Work.

The main things you will need to set up your Temple are as follows. An *Altar*: whether you utilise the double Cube of the Magicians or a decent sized coffee table is up to you and depends upon your aspiration. The Altar top can be elegant or left bare; however, you may need several *cloths* of different colours denoting the intent of the Ritual — the colours of the Elemental associations; black and white; spectrum colours; the colours of the Tree of Life and their attending Paths; planetary colours and/or different colours of Earth.

Upon your Altar will reside *Altar Candles* (see below) with *matches or tapers* to hand nearby, your *Censer* (Thurible, Incense Burner — other names for the same thing), your *Pentacle, Athame, Cup, Wand, dishes for Salt and Water*, your *Cords* (if necessary), your *Book(s)* with attending Work opened, and anything else that has been consecrated or that you consider sacred. You will also need to remember your *Grimoir* for the recording of any and all findings from your Ritual (and a *pen* with which to write them).

Remember to clear and clean everything within the proximity of your workspace.

You will need four *Candles*, each in its own candlestick, for the four Directions. These are set up within the boundary of the Circle. Your Altar is set to the South in the southern hemisphere, to the North in the northern lands — the place of Earth, the place of Midnight wherein all life-in-potential dwells. The Altar symbolises the Foundation of your Art and it is never ready until the Altar Candle is lit, as it represents the Light that dwells within all sacred environments and lights your way between the Worlds.

Before entering your Circle (the Temple is permanent once it is consecrated to your spiritual Path, whereas the Circle is created afresh each time you enter your Temple for a purpose), you are to bathe with the express purpose of cleansing away all that is of no significance to the Work at hand.

You are to prepare a jar of blended oils which will be consecrated for preparation of your body for entry into the Circle. It is best to use a base of either olive or sweet-almond oil (three-quarters of a jar), and add to it the essential oils that you are most attracted to, or that you feel represent your energies best. This jar of oil is kept in your bathroom but away from any other fingers that may decide to play around with it.

After you have indulged in your cleansing bath (to which it is good to add a little salt and a drop of oil) you are to oil your body with the consecrated oil and enter your Temple either naked or robed (depending on how you are most comfortable).

Hopefully you will have been observing the rising and the setting of the Sun and the Moon — this will enable you to have a direct link with the environment in which you dwell and assures that you do not become reliant on either things or habits, but rather on the tides of change to which our Planet resonates. You will set up your Altar as above and set the Elemental Candles accordingly.

Once your Temple is prepared and all things (including yourself) have been prepared to your observations and desire for perfection, you will enter into the Temple and begin to prepare to cast the Ritual Circle.

You are to light the Candle(s) upon your Altar as well as the Incense, and go into meditation before the Altar. It is advisable that you utilise either four-fold breathing or a soft humming-chant to focus and stabilise your energies prior to the Work of the Rite. When you are thoroughly focused you are to turn your Inner Sight to the task of seeing a beam of electric-blue light coming to you through the Inner Planes and encircling your

Sacred Space until it builds like a dome, spinning, always spinning in the direction of the Sun (anti-clockwise in the southern hemisphere, clockwise in the northern — sunwise being called 'Deosil'). When the image is substantial and fixed you will stand and circumambulate the Space, summoning the Forces of Life to aid and protect the place for the period of your Ritual. It is better to use words that are appropriate for you rather than read them by rote without any thought of what you say, as everything that is done within a Sacred Circle is to be done with intent. You are to continue to focus, with the Inner Sight, on the building spiral of Force that comprises the power of your Circle for the *whole* of the consecration.

Earth: When this is done you are to take the Altar Candle and are to go to the entrance of the Gate of Earth, light the Candle there and summon to the Guardian of that Place, as follows:

Come Ye, of the southern winds,
Place of storms and deepest Night,
Place of silence most profound,
And guard this Place,
Set outside of Time,
Acknowledge this Circle
Summoned in the Names of the Mistress and Master of all Living!
Open for me the Gate of Earth!

Draw, with your hand only at this stage, the Invoking Pentagram of Earth:

See before you a Gate of enormous proportions, entwined with ivy and morning glory. Your Pentagram acts as a sign to those that guard the Gate that you are aware and prepared, and so they will open it towards you. The scene behind the Gate is of vast primordial forests seen from within their depths. A Being will come through the forest towards you, either alone or attended by the Gnomes of Earth (Elementals), or the Sacred Animal of Earth, the Stag. The Being will match your Pentagram from their side of the Gate and will flood your Circle with a beam of deep green light.

Air: You will then move to the East, the entrance to the Gate of Air, and light the Candle and summon the Guardian of that Place, as follows:

Come Ye, of the East winds,
Place of the first Sunrise and the Rise of Moon,
Place of Inspiration,
And guard this Place,
Set outside of Time,
Acknowledge this Circle
Summoned in the Names of the Mistress and Master of all Living!
Open for me the Gate of Air!

Draw, with your hand only at this stage, the Invoking Pentagram of Air:

See before you a Gate of enormous proportions, made of silver and shimmering with light. Your Pentagram acts as a sign to those that guard the Gate that you are aware and prepared, and so they will open it towards you. The scene behind the Gate is as though you stood upon the highest mountain of the world and could see as far as forever. There are swiftly flying clouds and all the birds of the currents of Air fly around and beneath the sight. A Being will come towards you, dipping and riding the currents and tides, either alone or attended by the hosts of Sylphs (Elementals) of Air, or the Sacred Animal of Air, the Falcon. The Being will match your Pentagram from their side of the Gate and will flood your Circle with a beam of golden-yellow light.

Fire: You will then move to the North, the entrance to the Gate of Fire, and light the Candle and summon the Guardian of that Place, as follows:

Come Ye, of the northern winds,
Place of the highest Sun,
Place of Creation manifest
And guard this Place,
Set outside of Time,
Acknowledge this Circle
Summoned in the Names of the Mistress and Master of all
Living!
Open for me the Gate of Fire!

Draw, with your hand only, the Invoking Pentagram of Fire:

See before you a Gate of massive proportions, solid gold. Your Pentagram acts as a sign to those that guard the Gate that you are aware and prepared, and so they will open it towards you. The scene behind the gate is of a volcano as it is viewed from its lip, of Suns and Stars revolving in a dance about each other. A Being will come towards you from the heart of one of the Suns, either alone or attended by the Salamanders (Elementals) of Fire, or with the Sacred Animal of Fire, the Dragon. The Being will match your Pentagram from their side of the Gate and will flood your Circle with a beam of fiery-red light.

Water: You will then move to the West, to the entrance to the Gate of Water, and light the Candle and summon the Guardian of that Place, as follows:

Come Ye, of the West winds,
Place of the setting Sun,
Home of the Island Remembered,
Place of Wisdom,
And guard this Place,

Set outside of Time,
Acknowledge this Circle
Summoned in the Names of the Mistress and Master of all
Living!
Open for me the Gate of Water!

Draw, with your hand only, the Invoking Pentagram of
Water:

See before you a Gate of massive proportions, the metal algae-
green, the tides of ocean lapping at its base from the other side.
Your Pentagram acts as a beacon to those that guard the Gate
that you are aware and prepared, and so they will open it
towards you. Just behind the Gate are dark boulders that lead to
the ocean as far as the eye can see. There are creatures of the
oceans to be seen in all directions — whales and dolphins; great,
flat sting-ray; octopi; movement, arrow-shaped, as great schools
of fish travel their patterns. A Being will come towards you out
of the depths of this mighty Place, either alone or attended by
the hosts of Undine (Elementals) of Water, or with the Sacred
Animal of Water, the giant red Salmon. The Being will match
your Pentagram from their side of the Gate and will flood your
Circle with a beam of deep-blue light.

You will then return to your Altar and prepare for the
consecration of your Ritual things.

Consecration

Your first consideration is your Athame. This Tool is the
Witches' representation of Will and Intent and it acts as an
extension of the self. It is always double-edged, symbolic of the
Paths of Duality hereby represented as Compassion and
Severity.

To consecrate your Athame you will need to have the
following in your Circle with you: Wine; Cup; Salt and Water,
and the containers to hold the latter; some essential oil (musk

and jasmine are easily obtainable and mixed together they again symbolise the duality of masculine and feminine force); a white candle and your incense.

These things, along with your Athame, are placed upon your Altar whilst the preparations for the Ritual (casting the Circle, summoning the Guardians) take place.

Light the special white candle and raise your Athame, Blade pointed up, and call forth both the Moon Goddess and the Lord of Life in as many aspects as are valid to you, and ask that they bless the Blade of your Art. Draw the shape of the Invoking Pentagrams of Earth, Air, Fire and Water over the Athame, saying:

I invoke the Force of the Mighty Ones
To consecrate and charge this Blade
With universal Will!

Then take the Athame and hold it against your body, point down, and watch with your Inner Sight as light pours down, from the apex of your Circle, to entwine itself around both you and your Athame, directing the focus of light through the Blade and thence into your own body, where it will be seen as travelling in spirals through you and back out through the Blade, and upwards again through the apex of your Circle.

Take up your Athame and draw the sign of the Invoking Pentagram of Spirit (the same as the Pentagram of Earth except that the focal concentration is, from the topmost point and to subsequent points: 'From Spirit, to Earth, to Air, to Fire, to Water!') over the Salt and say:

Blessings be upon this Crystal of the Sea
Forced from the Womb of the Mother
By the might of the Sacred Sun!

Draw the sign of the Pentagram of Spirit over the Water and say:

Out of thee, Water creature,
Goes all that is not pure.
May only the essence remain!

Add the Salt to the Water and draw the sign of the Pentagram of Spirit upon your forehead with it, saying:

I work my Rite as Priest of the Ancient Way.
May the Gods see that which takes place here
And give blessings upon my chosen Path!

Work the Salt and Water into the Athame, Blade and Hilt.

Take the oil and draw the Pentagram of Spirit over it, saying:

I consecrate thee,
Essence of the living Plant,
Mayest thou aid me in my task!

Work the oil into your Athame, Blade and hilt.

Take the Cup of Wine and draw the Pentagram of Spirit over it, saying:

Thou art blessed,
Fruit of the Lord of the Earth!

Work the Wine into your Athame, Blade and hilt.
    Now take the Athame and pass it through the Flame of the Elemental Candle of Fire, saying:

The Element of Fire infuse my Blade!

Pass it through the Water and Salt, saying:

The Element of Water infuse my Blade!

Pass it through the Incense, saying:

The Element of Air infuse my Blade!

Then place the Athame, Blade down, upon the ground, saying:

The Element of Earth infuse my Blade!

Place your Athame against your chest and close your eyes,

concentrating all of your Will into it. Allow enough time to be absolutely certain that your objective has been met, then say:

Thou art mine!
I am thine!
We are One!

Kiss your newly consecrated Athame on both Blade and hilt and return it to your Altar.

The pattern for consecrations follows, generally, this format, but in future the Pentagrams (all of them) of summoning will be performed with your Athame in hand (it doubles the Will). Prior to Ritual use, and after, the Blade of your Athame is to be gently rubbed with a magnet to ensure its field of Force is maintained.

To Farewell the Guardians

Whatever purpose of intent you wish to pursue is undertaken whilst still in the Circle.

When you are done, you are to honour the Guardians through the act of farewell.

Earth You will proceed, firstly, to the Gate of Earth. Focus on the image of the Guardian standing sentinel at the open Gate (get your image clear!). Raise your arms, Athame in your right hand, and say:

I am allied to your Children of Earth
Wherever they may have need of me!
Accept me as one of the Children of Earth!
I give honour where it is due . . .
Great Powers of Earth
I salute You!

Draw the Banishing Pentagram of Earth with your Athame and watch as it disappears:

The Being who guards will acknowledge your Pentagram and close the Gate-Between-the-Worlds. They vanish from sight.
  Extinguish the Candle to the South.

Air Proceed to the Gate of Air. Focus on the Image of the Guardian standing sentinel at the open Gate. Raise your arms, Athame in your right hand, and say:

I am allied to your Children of Air
Wherever they may have need of me!
Accept me as one of the Children of Air!
I give honour where it is due . . .
Great Powers of Air
I salute You!

Draw the Banishing Pentagram of Air with your Athame and watch as it disappears:

The Being who guards will acknowledge your Pentagram and close the Gate-Between-the-Worlds. They vanish from sight.
  Extinguish the Candle to the East.

Fire Proceed to the Gate of Fire. Focus on the image of the Guardian standing sentinel at the open Gate. Raise your arms, Athame in your right hand, and say:

I am allied to your Children of Fire
Wherever they may have need of me!
Accept me as one of the Children of Fire!
I give honour where it is due . . .
Great Powers of Fire
I salute You!

Draw the Banishing Pentagram of Fire with your Athame and watch as it disappears:

The Being who guards will acknowledge your Pentagram and close the Gate-Between-the-Worlds. They vanish from sight.
  Extinguish the Candle to the North.

Water Proceed to the Gate of Water. Focus on the image of the Guardian standing sentinel at the open Gate. Raise your arms, Athame in your right hand, and say:

I am allied to your Children of Water
Wherever they may have need of me!
Accept me as one of the Children of Water!
I give honour where it is due ...
Great Powers of Water
I salute You!

Draw the Banishing Pentagram of Water with your Athame and watch as it disappears:

The Being who guards will acknowledge your Pentagram and close the Gate-Between-the-Worlds. They vanish from sight.
  Extinguish the Candle to the West.

To withdraw the Circle you walk against the Sun (clockwise, or 'Widdershins', in the southern hemisphere, anticlockwise in the northern), drawing the electric-blue light into the Blade of your Athame as you do so. When it is done you will raise your Athame Blade upwards and direct the energy in a line of Force towards the 'Roof of the World', where it will be taken up by the Evolving Whole for the sustenance of life where it is needed (which, currently, is just about everywhere!).
  When all is done then you will proclaim that:

The Rite is done! Blessed be!

Then, prior to Earthing yourself (see below), you will document in your Grimoir anything of importance that you were aware of during the Rite — do not miss anything, it may form a pattern as you progress. If you found harmony or invocation of your own or that was taken from inspiration during the Rite, then also take note of it so that, upon 'cleaning it up', you may enter it into your Book of Shadows.

Earthing

The process of Grounding or Earthing is imperative after working within your Circle.

Firstly, you are to rub your body down the arms, flick the energy off your hands; down your legs, flick the energy off your hands; down your torso and as much of your back as you can reach, flick the energy off your hands; over your face and head, flick the energy off your hands.

Secondly, you are to go and either drink down a full glass of water or eat some food (remember, you would not have done so for about three hours prior to the Work).

Thirdly, you are to immediately put away all of your Ritual things.

The Gates-Between-The-Worlds (Working Ritual)

The following four Rituals are worked independently of each other. You are to allow time between each working to enable you to be open to the influence of each working in your mundane experience of it. It is best if you work the rituals in the waxing cycle of the Moon each month (therefore allowing one month for the mundane, experiential part of the exercise).

Firstly you will be given a groundplan (revision time!) of each of the Elements. Learn them and expand upon them through personalised understanding as you go. Once you have become familiar with the associations you can proceed to the Ritual invocations of the Elemental Force, remembering to earth yourself after each working.

Every Ritual that you undertake *will* have an effect on your life — if you can keep that in mind throughout then you will be careful as to what you invoke (remember the Law of Cause and Effect).

There is a Legend (Pathworking) involved in each Ritual which you are to tape, in your own voice, prior to the working, so that you can travel through it — have the tape-recorder in the Circle with you. Those of you who find that learning through guided imagery is of benefit, and who wish to go further into not only our native tradition but those of Qabbalah, etc., will find a list of worthwhile texts in the Recommended Reading List on page 183.

Groundplan:
The Element of Earth
Environmental All solid matter, from the Earth Herself to the materials of both organic and inorganic matter, right down to the cellular level of all living things.
Personal Qualities We will generalise here and will achieve more if

we break down the qualities into positive and negative.

Positive Your own physical body is maintained at its maximum potential (less for the ego of having a 'beautiful' body as for the ability to perpetuate survival at its optimum); your ability to manipulate your financial situation so that you do not starve to death; your ability to organise at all levels of existence; your ability to manifest those things in your life that can otherwise remain only at inspiration point; all training methods that allow free expression of who you are (e.g. learning the ABC so that you can read, learning about colour, space, etc. if you wish to paint, and so on).

Negative The opposite of all the above.

Magical Represents the direction of South (in the southern hemisphere; North in the northern); the Archangelic Force is named Uriel; the Elemental King is named Ghobb; the Elementals are known as Gnomes; in the Qabbalah Earth represents the World of Assiah; the time of day ruling this Element is Midnight; the time of the Solar Year (in the southern hemisphere) is Winter Solstice; the Ritual Tool is the £Pentacle; of the Sacred Regalia the Weapon is the Shield.

The Element of Air

Environmental Oxygen; all gasses; atmospheric pressure; aerial currents; the winds that accompany them; the spaces between places.

Personal Qualities — Positive The intellect; inspiration; the ability to learn; the ability to be 'open' spiritually; the essence of both honour and co-operation; the quality of speech.

Negative The opposite of all the above.

Magical Represents the direction of East; the Archangelic Force is named Raphael; the Elemental King is named Paralda; the Elementals are known as Sylphs; in the Qabbalah Air represents the World of Yetzirah; the time of day ruling this Element is Dawn; the time of the Solar Year (in the southern hemisphere) is the Spring Equinox; the Ritual Tool is the Athame; of the Sacred Regalia the Weapon is the Sword.

The Element of Fire

Environmental Volcanic activity; the heat that warms our Planet; the Sun himself; lightning; electricity (in all its forms); the ion; all forms of flame; the heat that sustains life in the bodies of all living creatures.

Personal Qualities — *Positive* Spontaneity; excitement; lust; all creativity; the ability to manifest ideas into actions by the essence of personal 'drive'; the ability to inspire others through the spoken or the written word; sexuality; constructive anger.

Negative Apathy; all forms of violence; sloth; jealousy; spite.

Magical Represents the direction of North (in the southern hemisphere); the Archangelic Force is named Michael; the Elemental King is named Djinn; the Elementals are known as Salamanders; in the Qabbalah Fire is known as the World of Atziluth; the time of day ruling this Element is Midday; the time of the Solar Year is the Summer Solstice (southern hemisphere); the Ritual Tool is the Wand; of the Sacred Regalia the Weapon is the Staff.

The Element of Water

Environmental All liquids — the fluid parts of all living bodies; rain; dew; sap; oceans; rivers; subterranean waterways and lakes; mists and fog; clouds, etc.

Personal Qualities — *Positive* Love; compassion; awareness; co-operation; instinct; the transmutation of experience and learning into wisdom; psychic ability.

Negative The opposite of all the above, but we will include cynicism, sarcasm, alcoholism and all addictions including obsessions, spiritual naivety (i.e. sheep-consciousness).

Magical Represents the direction of West; the Archangelic Force is named Gabriel; the Elemental King is named Nixsa; the Elementals are Undines; in Qabbalah Water represents the World of Briah; the time of day ruling this Element is Sunset; the time of the Solar Year is Autumn Equinox (in the southern hemisphere); the Ritual Tool is the Cup; of the Sacred Regalia the Weapon is the Grail.

After absorbing all of the above associations (based on the *Book of Elements*), including those written up in the earlier part of this section, you are ready to flow with the Rituals of personal balancing (Elemental and Summoning) that will open your Doors of Priesthood.

Entering the Domain of Elemental Force

Before we begin it is necessary to understand the gift of the Gods to humanity — Creative Visualisation.

The 'rational' society of this and the last century has much to answer for when it tried (unsuccessfully) to belittle the greatest gift that the human mind has at its disposal — the imagination. This tool can be likened to several things: a transmitter and a receiver; a pool of inherited symbolic association; most important of all, a passport to the Realms of Dimension only hinted at by science — the Key to the Gates-Between-the-Worlds and our ability to walk within them!

The use of *controlled* Visualisation (rather than idle meandering) is wherein lies the Power of Magic. Understanding of symbolism, the language of Magic, the breaking down of conditioned apathy, the access of the Veil — all are the aims of the well trained Priest or Priestess of our Path. In all situations where known control is practised you will need to utilise your ability to 'look it up', when things other than those you have 'set up' come to you on your journeys.

The Domain of the Elements and the Beings that represent them are, at first consideration, easy to access — that 'ease', however, can be extremely misleading. Be wary of any egoistic interpretation of experience. The Elementals that inhabit their respective Realms are not, after all, human — this is the first thing to be understood; they do not 'think', they have no 'logical' processes, nor do they react in ways that we do. They simply *are*. They resonate to the Patterns and Laws of change-in-continuum that is Nature, but they are influenced by everything else that is subject to those same laws. For some inconceivable reason we, as a species, have virtually negated these laws and seek to control the patterns — this has led to the environmental madness that has virtually decimated our galactic home!

This denial of the Laws of Change has also come close to closing off the access to the Thresholds, and this process must not be perpetuated. For the denial of these Worlds would close down the inspiration necessary to amend the current decimation of our home (a little like the 'nothing' in the movie *The Never-Ending Story*).

Our ability to walk between the Worlds is our natural birthright. It is our personal responsibility as occultists to keep the doors open.

Through personalised understanding, through the Rituals, to alliance with these Elements and the inhabitants therein you pay honour to your own life by recognising the interconnectedness of the Whole. You will be summoning the Elemental Kings within the Rituals. They, unlike the Elementals that attend Them, *do* understand, *do* react. They are Beings of total intelligence of the patterns, and they can be either allies or enemies, depending on your true affiliations; they have had much to deal with since the advent of our industrial and technological revolutions, and they are not amused by those who seek self-glory through Magic at their expense, or the expense of the Dominions through which they rule.

We will begin with the Ritual of the Element of Earth, and work around the Circle through Air to Fire to Water in the Sunwise Cycle (the workings herein should cover the next four months of training). In the great northern lands you will work in similar sequence within the Sunwise Cycle in which you dwell, i.e. from North (Earth) to East (Air) to South (Fire) to West (Water), and you can continue to do so until you are at home with the significance, both personally and environmentally, of the Circle (at which time you can explore other possibilities — but that's another story), as the symbolism of Magic is very much like accessing a new and curious language.

The Ritual of Earth
(*The Alliance of Falias*)
Within your Circle you will require the following:

Ritual Tools

Pentacle; Athame; Wand; Cup; white Cord if you require the Boundary of your Circle in-manifest. You will need Salt and Water in their separate containers; Wine (within your Cup); five candlesticks, one will suffice for your Altar Candle and the other four for the Elemental Gateways; four bowls of earth (to be placed by the candles at the Elemental Gateways); your Robe (if you wish to work other than skyclad); a black, brown or dark green cloth onto which you either paint or sew the Hermetic symbol for the Element of Earth:

Also five dark-green candles; your Incense; consecrated oil; a fair-sized stone to represent the Lia-Fal (Stone of Truth) upon your Altar; your tape of the Inner Voyage, 'The Elemental Bear of Earth', plus your tape-player; matches to light the Candles and the Incense; have books and pen for recording your experience; a head-cloth.

Make certain that your Temple is clean and in readiness. Set up everything within the Temple and have all things upon the Altar that will be required during the Rite.

Bathe with intent of purification and oil your body.

Enter your Temple, light the Altar Candle to show that your Sacred Space is ready, and light the Incense (charcoal blocks that are self-igniting are available from your Catholic supply shop), and seat yourself before the Altar. Begin with four-fold breathing leading to a soft humming-chant until you are 'centred' (i.e. until nothing of your mundane life is within your thoughts).

When you are balanced you will stand and take your Athame in hand, kiss the Blade, draw from the Inner Planes the current of electric-blue light that will infuse your Blade, and begin your circumambulation of the Circle, weaving the light into a protective Force as you go. *Use your Inner Sight*, focus and controlled imagery being the operative expression of your Magical Will. When it is done and you can clearly 'see' it, you will return to your Altar, take up the Altar Candle and your Pentacle and proceed to the Gate of Earth.

Place the Altar Candle on the floor next to the point Candle, stand with Pentacle in your left hand and Athame in your right hand, close your eyes and visualise the Gateway there in front of you. When it is clearly seen, you say:

I summon the Guardian of the Gate of Earth!
Ghobb! King of the Powers of the South!
The Sacred Space is thine for this Night!
Open for me the Way-Without-Time.
Earth of Earth, I am One with thee!

Draw the Invoking Pentagram of Earth on the ether before you and see it complete in deep crystal-green. Wait and watch as the Gate opens.

Before you, on the other side of the Gate, you will see vast primordial forests, great boulders covered in lichens; you will smell the rich, loamy depths of the untouched forest; you will hear the muted sounds of wild things within the depths; you will feel the cool, moist air upon your face and hands.

There will come towards you a bear of a man, richly robed in the living foliage of the forest, vines and branches of living trees are upon his head. He will stride up to the open Gate and mirror your Pentagram and project it over to your side of the Gate, where it will stay, green fire, for the entirety of the Ritual. Light the Candle of the South and proceed around your Circle to the Gate of Air.

Place the Altar Candle on the floor beside the point Candle, keep the Pentacle in your left hand and Athame in your right, close your eyes and visualise the Gateway there in front of you. When it is clearly seen, you will say:

I summon the Guardian of the Gate of Air!
Paralda! King of the Powers of the East!
The Sacred Space is thine for this Night!
Open for me the Way-Without-Time.
Air of Earth, I am One with thee!

Draw the Invoking Pentagram of Air on the ether before you and see it complete in shimmering, pale-gold. Wait and watch as the Gate opens.

Before you, on the other side of the Gate, you will see from what appears to be the vantage point of a very high mountain, the swirling winds of a dawn sky, eagles rising on the tides of Air; swirling cloud, low on the horizon, tipped with beacons of dawn light; feel the crispness of the high altitude; smell the clarity of the Air; hear the roaring of the wind way down below in the valleys too far from here to be even imagined, and the call of birds as they glory in the birth of a new day.

There will come towards you a Being of Flight who will come to land on the pinnacle of the mountain. He will wear the colours of the clouds and the dawn. He will hold in his hands a Pentacle similar to your own to show you that he is fey with the Earth Realm. He will walk or fly to the open Gate. He will mirror your Pentagram and will project it over to your side of the Gate, where it will stay, gold-fire, for the entirety of the Ritual. Light the Candle of the East from the Altar Candle and proceed around your Circle to the Gate of Fire.

Place the Altar Candle upon the floor beside the point Candle, having the Pentacle in your left hand, the Athame in your right, close your eyes and visualise the Gateway there in front of you. When it is clearly seen, you will say:

I summon the Guardian of the Gate of Fire!
Djinn! King of the Powers of the North!
The Sacred Space is thine for this Night!
Open for me the Way-Without-Time.
Fire of Earth, I am One with thee!

Draw the Invoking Pentagram of Fire on the ether before you and see it complete in shimmering, rich red. Wait and watch as the Gate opens.

Before you, on the other side of the Gate, you will see a lake of volcanic flame. It is hot, very hot, not only due to the molten lake but also because the lake is in the unusual setting of an endless desert, the noon Sun, overhead, intense and blinding. Feel the heat on your skin, even from where you stand; smell the sulphur in the air; hear the fire and the plop-plopping of the lava as it breaks the surface of this entrance to the heart of the Earth-Mother.

A great and glorious flame will erupt from the Firelake and within its depths is a Being of radiant splendour. He comes towards you, clothed in the reds, oranges and yellows of his natural Domain, and one can never tell if his garment is ever still for it burns and burns but never burns! He mirrors your Pentagram and projects it over to your side of the Gate, where it will stay, glittering red, for the entirety of the Rite. Light the Candle of the North and proceed around your circle to the Gate of Water.

Place the Altar Candle on the floor beside the point Candle and raise the Pentacle and the Athame, as before, close your eyes and visualise the Gateway in front of you. When it is clearly seen, you will say:

I summon the Guardian of the Gate of Water!
Nixsa! King of the Powers of the West!
The Sacred Space is thine for this Night!
Open for me the Way-Without-Time.
Water of Earth, I am One with thee!

Draw the Invoking Pentagram of Water on the ether before you and see it complete in deep purple-blue, glowing like the blue within the crystal. Wait and watch as the Gate opens.

Before you, on the other side of the Gate, you will see what appears to be the heart of a mountain. It is not as dark as it would be if the phosphorescence was not glowing from the rock walls. The place is enormous, and cutting through the centre, weaving its way through stalagmites of ethereal beauty, is a river that rages through the cavern only to disappear down a cleft at the side of the Place. The river flows off to the sides of itself to form deep pools that await the unwary. Feel the chill of the ancient air; smell the scent of the water and rock; hear the raging of this mighty underground river.

The garment of the Being who comes out of the River is of waterfalls; the continuous flow goes ever back into the river of which it is a part — its rich deep blues and glinting lights telling of the depths from which it came. He comes towards you and stands at the other side of the Gate and mirrors your Pentagram, which is projected over to you, where it will stay for the entirety of the Ritual.

Light the Candle of the West with the Altar Candle and complete the Circle.

Return to your Altar, replace the Altar Candle, the Pentacle underneath it.

Take up the Water in its container, concentrate, place the Blade of your Athame within it and consecrate it thus:

Out of thee, Water creature,
goes all that is not pure!
May only the Essence of the Great Mother remain!

See, with your Inner Sight, the Water being infused with the electric-blue light from the tip of your Blade.

When it is charged, replace it upon the Altar and take up the vessel of Salt. Place the tip of your Blade into it, concentrate, and say:

Blessings be upon thee, symbol of Earth,
Forced from the Womb of the Mother
By the might of the Sacred Sun!

See, again with your Inner Sight, the Salt being infused with the light of your Will. When it is charged you will add it to the Water and stir them both together. You will take some of it onto your finger and draw the Pentagram of Spirit upon your forehead (to open you to your own Priesthood) before replacing the container upon the Altar.

Now take up your Cup (the Wine will already be in it) and place your Athame Blade therein. Concentrate on the symbolism of this for a moment (the symbolic uniting of God and

Goddess). Draw from the tip of your Blade the power of your Will and see it merge with this union. When you feel it happening, you will say:

The Cup is the symbol of Woman and my Goddess!
The Athame is as Man and my God!
Co-joined they are the Blessed Union
That produces the Three Drops of Inspiration,
The Creation continuous!

Replace your Athame upon the Altar, raise the Cup and offer it to your Goddess and God as a gesture of your understanding and alliance, and drink from the cup, in full understanding of what you do.

Now you will sit upon the cloth that you have prepared and touch each of its corners (the perimeter, if it is circular) with the consecrated Water and Salt. You will then spend time meditating on *all* the aspects of Earth that you can consider, both environmentally and personally. Understand yourself as an evolving part of the pattern. Try not to just 'surface think' the associations, but pull them down within the self so that they are not just understood but absorbed.

Make certain that the Censer is still glowing and refuel it with Incense. Place the tape-player within reach for when the chant is done, and place the head-cloth over your head.

Begin your deep breathing again and feel the Forces build around you. Have the chant memorised prior to the Ritual. When your breathing has built to a peak you begin the chant, which is to be repeated over and over until it 'takes' you:

By the Dance
And in the Darkness
By the Door and by the Drum
By Enchantment
The Eye of Midnight,
The Inner Shield
I bid thee come!

When you are 'taken' you can free-flow on the Inner Planes until it is time to leave.

Breathe softly to lessen the effect of your power-raising, then switch on the tape-player and go with the flow of the Legend until it is finished.

*   *   *

The Legend of the Bear of Earth

'Let me take you on a journey into the future; through yesterday's indifference and today's fear; through tomorrow's despair and, finally, into the hope of eternity. Let me tell you the Legend, not of a time that was but of a time that may be . . . of a man such as you once were, and are, and can be.

Listen and I will tell you of the Lost Children of Earth. Listen and weep.

The cave seemed a haven of warmth as Kesh staggered in from the savage, white blizzard that raged across the barren landscape outside. He fell clumsily to his knees, his breath rasping cruelly into lungs seared raw by the icy bitter wind. Though robed and wrapped from head to foot there was little of warmth left anywhere in this man. Vicious pellets of ice, driven by the unearthly wind, had penetrated every fold and seam of his worn and weathered attire, his beard and moustache were frozen solid and he had long since lost all feeling in his fingers and toes. With the last of his failing strength he struggled out of his outer garments and shrugged them to the floor, where they lay heavy and stiff with deeply encrusted snow and ice.

There was a deep, dry litter of twigs and dirt on the floor of the cave and Kesh burrowed thankfully into it. He lay long, covered thus, waiting for the bone-wrenching spasms of shaking to pass, and for his shattered wits to restore themselves to some semblance of order. Outside the blizzard shrieked and screamed and howled like a wild beast cheated of its prey. As his breath slowed and evened out, however, Kesh became chillingly aware of another, slower rhythm, also within the cave. Holding his breath altogether for a moment, the man listened intently.

Yes! There it was! The unmistakable sound of the slow and

steady breathing of a large, sleeping animal. In the dim light that penetrated into the cave from the outside he could see the still, hulking form of a huge brown bear. How had this creature survived the desolation of the landscape and all within it? How did it now survive when all else was dead? These thoughts flew through Kesh's numbed brain as he lay considering probability against possibility. Answers found he none, but one thing he knew for sure: only a man tired of living would willingly tangle with a hibernating bear. Kesh was not tired of living, but he was awfully tired of dying.

After a moment's thought he decided to take his chances in the cave with the bear rather than commit certain suicide by returning to the blizzard outside. Indeed, it could well be that the bear meant the difference between life and death to Kesh. Already he could feel the living warmth of the animal penetrating his frozen, pain-wracked body.

Slowly, cautiously and ever so quietly the man stripped the last of his garments from his body. He then spread them out on the floor to dry, staying well clear of the dark shape that was the sleeping hulk of bear outlined against the far wall. His cloak, hood and boots were frozen stiff and would become saturated with the melting ice and snow before they could begin to dry out. Kesh was in for a long wait before he could leave the cave and continue his journey, and the presence of the bear did not promise to make the wait seem any the shorter.

A fire was obviously out of the question, even though there was fire-making equipment in the man's worn pack, so he withdrew from it instead a small portion of his dried travelling food. Sleep found him, however, curled up in a tight ball, hugging his cold body and legs, with trembling arms, before the food even made its way to his mouth.

Outside, the ravenous wind bit and tore with icy teeth, devouring the warmth and life of every living thing in its path. Kesh lay in a feverish sleep, haunted by dreams of a towering, white monster, breathing ice and snow, that stalked him through a maze of dark tunnels with a huge brown bear at its heels.

He woke suddenly, his eyes wide and staring and his heart pounding. The storm raged on unabated outside and Kesh strained to hear the sound that had awoken him above the howling gale. His eyes caught a slight movement at the rear of the cave. "By all the . . . Oh no, please no!" his thoughts were frantic, "Surely not . . . you can't wake up now!"

Moving only his eyes Kesh judged the distance between himself, the bear and the mouth of the cave. He could make it outside before the bear reached him — just — but without his heavy wraps and boots he would die within the hour in the freezing wind that could turn a man's very blood and marrow to ice. Mentally juggling the relative merits of death by freezing against death by bear, the man crouched, dry mouthed and trembling, and waited for the animal to make its move.

Slowly the bear sat up on its haunches and gazed steadily towards the man who had dared to intrude upon his winter sleep. Kesh stared back, willing the animal to lay down again and return to sleep. It did not. Rather, it raised its paws to its huge head — and pushed! The head slipped backwards revealing, beneath, the face and grey-haired skull of a very old man. This ancient being smiled toothlessly at Kesh, the many folds of his dry, dark skin crinkling around his black, bright eyes. He was squatting amongst the dry litter that had been the bear's bed, his skeletal legs folded under him and his gaunt knees poking forwards. His long bony arms rested on his thighs, fingers like old, dry twigs dangling loosely between his legs.

Around him lay several objects that bespoke his calling, and Kesh regarded these in puzzlement for some considerable time. Realisation dawned slowly as he recognised first the Shaman's drum, though the symbols painted thereon meant nothing to Kesh. There was also an intricately decorated rattle lying by the old one's feet, and before him rested a long, powerful staff, hung with feathers, small pouches and other mysterious trappings. Around the ancient neck hung a row of long, yellow, bear's teeth, and his chest and arms were covered in delicate tattoos of blue. He wore the entire skin of a bear, its head covering his and the wicked, curved claws dangling over his hands.

Taking a long, whistling breath the Shaman spoke to Kesh in a voice surprisingly rich and deep. "The earth sleeps as winter rules, and the bear dreams in midnight's dark blanket. Why then do the Children cry, and call to me from their tomb? Whose hand has sealed them up in living death? Whose hand will set them free? The Children cry and whisper in my dreams and will not let me sleep!"

Kesh stared uncomprehendingly at the old man, trying to make some sense of his strange words. Then, as if in response to some hidden signal, the cave became filled with the sounds of soft, anguished whisperings. Like the muffled pleas of children in great pain the murmurings and crying rolled round and round the cave, echoing off the walls and collecting in the corners like dry, rustling leaves. The Shaman hunched his shoulders and bent his head in an attitude of great despair, while Kesh clapped his hands to his ears and shut his eyes tightly in an attempt to keep out the terrible, haunting sounds.

Eventually they faded until only the faintest whispers and whimpered words drifted up from the depths of the Earth. Try as he might Kesh could not but recognise a single sound that alone was clear amongst the confused cacophony — and that one sound struck cold and fearful at his heart: "Kesh! Kesh! Kesh!" the pleading voices called his name.

The Shaman took up his drum and began to play a soft, complex rhythm, as Kesh moved in agitation around the cave, looking for a possible source of the heart-wrenching sounds. He barely noticed the insistent, hypnotic drum-beat spinning cobwebs in his head until finally he stood, entranced, before a large, dark crack that rent the wall at the back of the cave. The anguished murmurs rose up to meet him from deep within the Earth, tugging and pulling at him like little trembling fingers to draw him down into the chilling blackness.

Kesh had stepped into the fissure before he realised it, his body shivering with a chill that his mind did not register. His eyes were closed yet he perceived his surroundings clearly as if lit by a soft, diffused light.

The rock was dark and damp and grey, marbled with lighter

streaks and occasionally broken with a black, jagged crack. His downward path wove and twisted through cold hard rock which gave way to dark, moist earth in places, crumbling damply as he passed. He met with the huge gnarled roots of ancient trees which seemed to reach out and touch him with rough, fibrous fingers as he passed. He marvelled at their presence, deeply hidden underground, for the tall green trees that they had once supported were long gone from the empty, barren land above.

With each step the desperately sad sounds of little children weeping grew stronger and Kesh moved forward as quickly as he possibly could, feeling for every turn and twist in the narrow path he followed. The way was rough indeed, with no aspect of the tight, dark tunnel being constant or predictable. The sides widened and narrowed abruptly, while the ceiling, likewise, rose and fell treacherously. Time and again Kesh lost his footing as the rock below his feet dropped suddenly, tripping him the next moment as it jutted up again. His head was bleeding from a deep cut inflicted when the roof of the tunnel had fallen suddenly, and his tortuous progress was made worse by the plaintive sobs and whispers that tormented his every moment.

At one place Kesh was amazed to see around him a soft, golden glow. There was a broad band of humming, vibrant light running across his path. He was able to follow its course, more by feel than by sight, in either direction, marvelling at the power and energy that throbbed and pulsed within the glow; as he stepped into it he felt the shock of awareness course through his body, and every fibre of his being hungered for the touch of the ancient Ley-line to go on and on forever — yet within that path of power the voices were even stronger and more insistent, and the pain of them tore at his heart and screamed in his mind. He stepped out of the light and shivered.

The tunnel along which he had been irresistibly drawn came abruptly to an end at a roughly hewn stone door. With horror Kesh now not only heard the cries and sobs but the unmistakable sound of little fingers tearing and scrabbling at cold, unyielding rock. He raised a trembling hand to the door but it swung open while his touch was still a hair's breadth away.

The sight that met his reluctant gaze caused his heart to leap wildly to his mouth, then drop to his breast again as cold as stone. The door opened onto a large round chamber, the walls of which were smooth and translucent, lit from behind by some unearthly light. Behind the walls, *within* the walls, were hundreds of tiny forms, writhing and struggling against their living entombment. Kesh walked slowly around the room, eyes wide and teeth clenched painfully. Occasionally he put out a hand to touch the unyielding rock walls. When he did there were always at least a half-a-dozen other, smaller hands reaching imploringly towards his.

"Who *are* you?" he cried.

A small, solemn-eyed, shaggy-haired figure moved forward behind the imprisoning wall. He appeared to be as a boy-child, though his skin was hued with green and his hair was rough and mossy. "We are the Children of the Earth," he spoke softly, large shimmering tears rolling down his elfin face. "I was a Child of the Moor," he continued, "of the wild, rolling lands that swept greenly across the face of our Mother." He began to sob uncontrollably. "I remember the feel of the wind and the sun," he cried, "I remember . . .". His voice rolled into a wail and filled the chamber with unspeakable pain.

One tiny form with huge black eyes and soft, fluffy, snow-white fur covering its body reached out a hand towards Kesh. "I was the Seal-Child," she murmured, "mine was the spirit that rode the waves and knew the deep, green underwater world of wonder! Oh, how the Mother loved to see us play! Then . . . then . . .". Suddenly she screamed and Kesh watched frozen with horror as her head exploded into a bright, bloody mass and the soft white fur began to peel away from her body.

He turned his head, only to catch the eye of another weeping form kneeling behind the opaque wall and tearing at it with broken, bleeding fingers. "My People were the tall, green trees whose tops towered above the Earth and were home to many of my brothers and sisters here. Old, old we were, old as time itself.

We were born into a time of peace and beauty when men lived as One with the Mother." Despite her tears her eyes took on a cold, hard glint. She raised her finger at Kesh. "Look upon that which you have wrought!" she cried, "Look you now upon the work of man!" She resumed the futile task of clawing at the stone.

One by one other little forms came forward, some speaking softly, others crying out in heart-stopping wails of anguish. "I was a Child of the Deer . . .". "Mine were the Gentle People of the Streams . . .". "Of Flowers was I born, sweet and fragrant . . .", and all the while the cries and sobs assaulted Kesh like living blows. He felt panic and desperation bubbling deep within him; his head reeled, his body trembled, his heart pounded painfully. Never had he dreamed that such pain and sorrow was possible, never had the heart and soul of one man been subjected to such a plight as these tortured, little Children of Earth presented.

With a howl he threw himself at the walls, thrashing and pounding, with every ounce of desperate strength. It availed him not, though the wide-eyed Children beyond pressed forward eagerly, faces still and intent. Hope shone in every strange, magical eye; blind hope, desperate hope, futile hope.

The walls cared nothing for Kesh's assault. The wicked, heartless power that had driven Earth's Children deep into Her womb entombed them, living, in the hard, relentless stone, held them fast. Strength spent, Kesh fell to his knees and pressed his broken, bloody, wrecked hands against the rock. He held his face against the wall that separated him from the now quiet Children and his hot tears fell upon the cold stone.

Slowly, so slowly, imperceptibly at first, the tears he shed worked their way into the rock. Where all else had failed, each bitter tear wrung from Kesh's grieving heart dissolved a tiny part of that cold cruel wall . . .

Yet should he cry for a hundred years (and well he might) this one man's tears alone will not crumble it away.

The cave lives within the destiny of us all. The bear, grizzled Guardian of the Way to the Heart of the Mother, awaits us. He will beat the drum for all of us if we but dare to seek him out and rouse him from his troubled sleep.'

* * *

At the end of the Ritual you will take up the consecrated oil and rub the Stone with it — it is then to be considered as a Sacred Symbol representing your own Truth, and can be left placed at the Gate of Earth or by your Altar from this night onwards — it is also to remind you of your allegiance.

To complete your Ritual you will give thanks to the Lord and Lady of all living. You go, then, back to the Gate of Earth and see the Being standing sentinel there. Have your Athame with you and raise it to the Guardian and say:

Powers of Earth,
Place of deepest Night,
Guardian of the Gate I pledge my Earth to thine!
Depart in peace to whence ye came
Until we meet again!

Draw the Banishing Pentagram on the ether and watch as the Being mirrors it from the other side of the Gate. See him go, and watch as the Gate closes. With the tip of your Blade you will extinguish the Candle there.

Go to the East. See the Being standing sentinel. Raise your Athame in salute to the Guardian and say:

Powers of Air,
Place of Dawn,
Guardian of the Gate I pledge my Air to thine!
Depart in peace to whence ye came
Until we meet again!

Draw the Banishing Pentagram of Air upon the ether and watch as the Being mirrors it from his side of the Gate. See him go, and watch as the Gate closes. With the tip of your Blade extinguish the Candle there.

Go to the North. See the Being standing sentinel at the Gate. Raise your Athame in salute and say:

Powers of Fire,
Place of the Highest Sun,
Guardian of the Gate I pledge my Fire to thine!
Depart in peace to whence ye came
Until we meet again!

Draw the banishing Pentagram of Fire upon the ether and watch as the Being mirrors it from his side of the Gate. See him go, and watch as the Gate closes. With the tip of your Blade you will extinguish the Candle of the North.

Go to the West. See the Being standing sentinel there. Raise your Athame in salute to the Guardian and say:

Powers of Water,
Place of the Setting Sun,
Guardian of the Gate I pledge my Water to thine!
Depart in peace to whence ye came
Until we meet again!

Draw the Banishing Pentagram of Water on the ether before you, and watch as the Being mirrors it from the other side of the Gate. See him go, and watch as the Gate closes. Extinguish the Candle of the West with the tip of your Athame Blade.

Complete the Circle by continuing until you stand back at the South (North in the northern lands); focus intent, and using your Athame draw the electric-blue light of the Circle proper back into the Blade, and from there direct the Force to the Inner Planes to aid you in building your Inner Temple.

The Ritual of Air
(*The Alliance of Gorias*)
Within your Circle you will require the following:

Ritual Tools
Athame; Wand; Pentacle; Cup; white Cord (if you require the boundary of your Circle in-manifest); Salt and Water, each in their separate containers; Wine, within your Cup; five candlesticks, one for the Altar and the other four for the Gateways; your Robe if desired; a pale blue, yellow or white cloth onto which you will either paint or sew the Hermetic symbol of Air:

Also, five yellow candles; your Incense; consecrated oil; your tape of the Inner Voyage, 'The Elemental Bird of Air', plus the tape-player; matches to light the Candles and Incense; your book and pen for recording your experience; a head-cloth.

Make certain that your Temple is clean and in readiness. Set up everything within your Temple and have all things upon your Altar that will be required during the Rite.

Bathe with intent of purification and oil your body.

Enter your Temple, light the Altar Candle to indicate that your Sacred Space is ready, and light the Incense. Seat yourself before the Altar, begin your four-fold breathing leading to the soft humming-chant until you are centred.

When you are balanced you will stand and take your Athame in hand, kiss the Blade, draw from the Inner Planes the electric-blue light that will infuse your Blade, and begin to circumambulate your Circle, weaving the blue light into a strong protective force as you go. *Use your Inner Sight*. Focus and control. When it is done and you can see it, you will return to your Altar, take up the Altar Candle and the Incense and proceed to the Gate of Air.

Place the Altar Candle and the Incense on the floor beside the point Candle, stand with Athame in hand, close your eyes and visualise the Gate there in front of you. When it is clearly seen, you say:

I summon the Guardian of the Gate of Air!
Paralda! King of the Powers of the East!
The Sacred Space is thine for this Night!
Open for me the Way-Without-Time.
Air of Air, I am One with thee!

Draw the Invoking Pentagram of Air on the ether before you and see it complete in shimmering pale gold. Wait and watch as the Gate opens.

Before you, on the other side of the Gate, you will see the Earth below you, as though you were a bird-of-prey; there is nothing to support you, you feel the power of flight within your very being! Your vision is unimpeded from horizon to horizon — your sight is incomparable! Feel the tides of Air assist you to hover without apparent movement; your sense of smell keeps you in constant touch with the wind-moods and the patterns of the weather; from the vantage point of great height you can hear what prey moves upon the earth far below.

There will come towards you a Being of Flight who wears the colours of the Dawn — he holds, in both his hands, a bejewelled Sword that appears cast of the colours of the stars.

He will soar to the Gate and mirror your Pentagram and project it over to your side of the Gate, where it will stay, pale-gold fire, for the entirety of the Ritual. Light the Candle of the East and proceed around your Circle to the Gate of Fire.

Place the Altar Candle and the incense on the floor beside the point Candle, raise your Athame in summoning, close your eyes and visualise the Gateway in front of you. When it is clearly seen, you will say:

I summon the Guardian of the Gate of Fire!
Djinn! King of the powers of the North!
The Sacred Space is thine for this Night!
Open for me the Way-Without-Time
Air of Fire, I am One with thee!

Draw the Invoking Pentagram of Fire on the ether in front of you, and see it complete in shimmering, vibrant red. Wait and watch as the Gate opens.

Before you, on the other side of the Gate, you will see great expanses of outback desert; the sky is clear but the wind is strong, dry and very hot — almost crisping in its intensity; feel the intense dryness on your skin; smell the ozone in the air; taste the faint metallic taste that has settled on your lips and watch the grandeur and power of an electrical storm off on the northern horizon; and hear, as you run your fingers through your hair, the crackle of static that attends such majestic phenomenon.

There will come towards you a Being of awesome beauty and strength. He wears the colours of pale yellow and white that signify his understanding of Fire and Air. He holds in his hands a bolt of lightning in the semblance of a Sword to signify that he is fey with the Realms of Air. He stands at your open Gate. He will mirror your Pentagram and project it over to your side of the Gate, where it will burn without burning for the entirety of the Ritual. Light the Candle of the North from the Altar Candle and proceed around your Circle to the Gate of Water.

Place the Altar Candle and the Incense on the floor beside the point Candle, raise your Athame in summoning with your right hand, close your eyes and visualise the Gateway there in front of you. When it is clearly seen, you will say:

I summon the Guardian of the Gate of Water!
Nixsa! King of the Powers of the West!
The Sacred Space is thine for this Night!

Open for me the Way-Without-Time.
Water of Air, I am One with thee!

Draw the Invoking Pentagram of Water on the ether before you and see it complete in deep purple-blue. Wait and watch as the Gate opens.

Before you, on the other side of the Gate, you will see a landscape shrouded in moving, swirling mist; feel it brush your body with its damp kiss; hear the muted sounds of water dripping from indistinct shapes; smell the moisture on the dusk air.

A Being will come towards you clothed in the blue-grey colours of mist close to the ocean. He holds in his hands that which could only be described as 'the Sword of Illusion' — he is the authority of choice and discernment (the Qabbalistic Yesod) and in seeing Him you will be aware that there are very distinct but fine lines, and ofttimes very little difference to all appearances, between true Walking Between the Worlds and the illusions engendered by the emotional needs of those who would seek the Doorways as a support (in reality it should be the other way around).

He stands at the open Gate. He will mirror your Pentagram and will project it over to your side of the Gate, where it will glow in an almost gun-metal blue for the entirety of the Ritual.

Light the Candle of the West from the Altar Candle, take the Incense back to the Altar as well as the Altar Candle, refuel your Censer.

Take up the Water in its container, place the Blade of your Athame within it, concentrate on pulling the Force down the Blade and consecrate it thus:

Out of thee Water creature,
Goes all that is not pure!
May only the Essence of the Great Mother remain!

See, with the Inner Sight, the Water being infused with the electric-blue light of the Inner Planes that emanates from your Blade. When it is charged replace it on the Altar, take up the Salt in its container and pour it onto the Pentacle. Place the tip of your Blade in it and say:

Blessings be upon thee, Symbol of Earth
Forced from the Womb of the Mother
By the might of the Sacred Sun!

See, again with your Inner Sight the Salt being infused with the light of your Will. When it is charged you will add it to the Water and stir them both together. Take some of it onto your finger and draw the sign of the Pentagram of Spirit upon your forehead before replacing the container back upon the Altar.

You now take up the Cup of Wine and place your Athame Blade within it. Concentrate on the symbolism. Draw from the tip of your Blade the power of your Will and see it merge with the Union. When it is done, you will say:

The Cup is the Symbol of Woman and my Goddess!
The Athame is the Symbol of Man and my God!
Co-joined they are the Blessed Union
That produces the Three Drops of Inspiration,
The Creation continuous!

Raise the Cup and offer it to your Goddess and God as a gesture of your alliance, then drink from the Cup in full understanding of what you do (and if you do not, then read over the Invocation again and meditate upon it — the answer will be obvious).

Now seat yourself upon the cloth that you have prepared and touch each of its corners with the consecrated Water (the perimeter if it is circular). Now spend time meditating on all the aspects of Air that you can, both environmentally and personally. Know yourself as an evolving part of the Great Pattern. Do not just 'think' the associations, but pull them deeply down within yourself so that they are absorbed and not just comprehended.

Ascertain that the Censer is still well alight and refuel it if necessary. Place the tape-player where you can reach it when you have raised the chant, and place the head-cloth over your head.

Begin your deep breathing again and feel the Forces build around you.

Have the chant memorised prior to the Ritual until it is automatic. When your breathing has built to a peak you begin the chant, which is to be repeated over and over until it 'takes' you:

By the Bridge that spans the River;
By the Book — the Shadow Tome;
By the Breath, the Sword of Wisdom,
By Tuatha'n Bow
I bid thee come!

When you are 'taken' you can free-flow on the Inner Planes until it is time to leave. Breathe softly to lessen the effects of your power-raising, switch on the tape-player and go with the flow of the Legend until it is finished.

*   *   *

The Legend of the Bird of Air

'The Hawk shifted painfully on her perch as the leather thonging around her leg chafed cruelly. Hunger and thirst burned in her body, as fear and hatred burned in her soul. Properly named a Gyrfalcon, her capture had been the cause of great excitement and self-congratulation between the lord of the castle and his hawkmaster. By royal decree the Gyrfalcon was preserved for the King's personal and exclusive use. The lesser nobility flew Peregrines, while the sporting priesthood were given the Kestrel with which to hunt. The carefully structured and rigidly enforced hierarchy extended even to the birds and animals that one might keep in one's mews and stables. The snaring of the Gyrfalcon (a young bird exhausted from her arduous winter journey from the Arctic Circle) represented a small victory in the young lord's ongoing rebellion against his king.

But now it seemed the victory was turning sour as the bird, by means of her own death, was about to snatch it from them. Almost seventy-two hours had elapsed since her capture in the net, to the incredulous joy of Malcolm, the hawkmaster, and Finbar, his apprentice.

The bird was snowy-white, in her winter plumage, her eyes yellow and fierce. She was a magnificent size, especially considering that she was not yet fully grown; almost two feet long from beak-tip to tail-end, even the experienced hawkmaster had had a mighty struggle to hold her and get her back to the castle. Once secure in the mews, Malcolm had fought the furious bird; first to get the jesses on her legs, then to get the soft leather rufter over her head, and finally to get her onto the block. She resisted frenziedly with her long, hooked beak. The hawkmaster, famed for his skill, had begun the painstaking process of training straight away, but the bird would have none of it. Every method he knew, and some he had just invented, failed miserably as the beautiful Gyrfalcon sat starving on her block.

Finally his patience, under pressure from his own expectations and those of his lord, snapped. He stalked from the mews, hurling the raw meat he had been holding out for the bird into the midden, in a violent gesture of disgust. In an uncharacteristic outburst he cuffed the apprentice Finbar and ordered him to the kitchen for more fresh offal. "Get that bird to eat, dammit! Earn your keep!" he raged, "Or I'll throttle both you and it before I'm a day older, I swear!" In impotent rage he hammered his fist again and again against the stable wall, causing the animals inside to snort and jump in alarm.

Finbar, steaming offal in his gloved hand, judiciously emptied his bladder before entering the mews. He had stood many times before a bird in training and knew well the limitations of his body and the stresses placed upon it. For this reason, also, he made certain that he had a bucket of water and a dipper to hand. Of food he had none and must needs do without for however long this took.

His heartbeat quickened and his hand trembled as he stood and looked at the Gyrfalcon. How could he hope to succeed where his master had failed? Indeed, the bird that had seemed so magnificent but three short days ago now looked a pitiful sight. Her head drooped and her beak was slightly parted as she strove for breath through her terrible thirst and fear. Her feathers looked dull and untidy and she turned her head as far as she could away from the now smelly mess of raw meat which had been left on her block.

For the first time ever Finbar was appalled at the ordeal that the wild-caught birds underwent. He was by now adept at training an eyas, a fledgeling stolen from the nest, and had eagerly anticipated his graduation to the captured free-birds. He had, in fact, made an auspicious beginning with several Peregrines, which now sat, tamed and obedient, under their hoods in the darkening mews. But this beautiful, snow-white creature before him awakened an entirely new emotional response in him. Although already familiar with the rapport he was able to establish with the birds in his care, he was entirely unprepared for the flood of sensation that came to him in waves from the Gyrfalcon. He could feel her rage and despair beat upon him like a palpable force. Her dreadful hunger and thirst, coupled with her utter revulsion of the dead meat beside her, assailed his senses. Moreover, his heartfelt sympathy and respect for the bird made his task now seem cruel and degrading.

Forgetting all his training he crooned a low endearment to the Gyrfalcon as she watched him balefully, and then moved forward to stroke her breast with a softly held feather. Instantly he realised his mistake, but it was too late. With an exultant scream the bird dove forward, jabbing with incredible power her sharp, hooked beak into Finbar's face. His cry was muffled by the hands he held up to the agony and through which dark blood now bubbled and ran. She had struck his eye. He slumped unconscious to the straw-covered floor and lay as still as death. The Gyrfalcon eyed him dispassionately.

Finbar woke to the feel of cool wind blowing fresh in his face, smelling of sea and sun and snow. His eyes were closed and he feared to try to open them, knowing that one was surely lost. However, he felt no pain and in bewilderment he tried to raise

91

his hand to touch the injured part. The movement of his arm and hand felt all wrong, and with a wildly beating heart he opened his eyes and turned to look.

He had no hand, nor arm, and stared in amazement at what he saw — a long, white wing lay by his side, each single feather beautifully formed and shaped, the whole structure an absolute perfection. The wind ruffled his feathers, and Finbar felt his whole body respond to it with a sweet yearning and an intense desire to be at one with the Air currents around him.

"I am dead!" he thought, "Surely this is death!"

"No," replied a soft voice within his head, "but perhaps now you will discover what it means to *live*."

Finbar started. "Who are you?" he asked, "*Where* are you?"

"I am Ysulka," the voice answered, "the Gyrfalcon. Bird of the snow and the wind and the hunt. I am where you are and you are where I am, and we are wherever we choose to be!"

Finbar did not understand, but somehow it seemed inappropriate and unnecessary to say so.

"My freedom is lost to me," the voice went on, "and my life, too, will soon be gone. I, at least, know what it is I have lost and why I would sooner die than live without it. You, my friend, will die, as you have lived, grovelling in the dirt and darkness, a slave to your need to bind and hold and tame that which you envy and cannot emulate! Come," she said, "let me teach you how to *live* before I show you how to die!"

So saying, the other awareness in his head, that which was Ysulka, moved the wings of the body they were sharing and launched them into the Air. They had been perched on the branch of a gnarled, twisted old tree growing almost at the very edge of a cliff. The cliff fell away, sheer and steep, to a wide snow-covered plain below. They soared effortlessly upwards on a swirling current of Air which rose from the land and moved along the cliff-faces.

The Sun was rising, a bright golden orb in a crystal sky streaked with yellows, pinks, white and the palest of blues. There were exciting scents of spring on the wind, and Finbar, with the Gyrfalcon's heightened senses, smelled the new life surging and bursting in the trees. He caught the scents of the very early spring flowers pushing through the snow. He smelled the thawing ice gushing into swollen streams and the rich, moist earth beneath it all.

He smelled animals returning north again — deer, wolves, shaggy bovines; a myriad of birds — incredibly their scents came clear and strong, each individual and distinct. Neither had Finbar ever dreamed that hawks could hear like this: from the booming and cracking of far-distant monoliths of ice to the warning cries of tiny animals scurrying to safety below them.

He could hear it all borne on the wind . . . the wind! The magic of the wind! The wind that carried them high above the Earth, supporting them and caressing them, taking them on flights of sheer joy. The wind, divine messenger, that carried all the sights and sounds and smells of life itself to those who knew how to listen and see! The wind that blew from one end of the Universe to the other, gathering to itself the wisdom and knowledge of all Creation. Every sight and smell and sound that ever was, was swept up and carried aloft, blowing about the heavens and spiralling upwards to infinity. The wind was a God, and the mighty birds who knew its secrets were its Priesthood! Finbar exulted as they dove and swooped, soared and floated, rose high on mighty wing-beats and drifted slowly down again.

Against the whiteness of the snow Finbar and Ysulka's exquisitely sensitive eyes caught the movement of a ptarmigan, still in its white winter plumage. They dropped like a stone towards the earth, wings back, head down and talons thrust forward. A scream tore from their throat an instant before they struck. A kill! Ripping and tearing the soft, warm flesh, Finbar felt the hot spurt of blood fill their mouth and knew the sweet taste of death, and life.

He heard Ysulka laugh in his mind.

Finbar moaned softly and tried to move. An incredible bolt of pain shot through his eye and into his head. His mouth was swollen and dry and filled with his own cold, sticky blood. His mind felt numb as he tried to reorient his consciousness from Finbar/Ysulka to Finbar the boy. He slowly opened his good eye, where he lay, and sought Ysulka's outline in the dark mews. A movement in the straw nearby caught his attention, and ignoring the terrible pain he moved swiftly to grab the rat. Wringing its neck he stumbled towards the Gyrfalcon. "Eat, Ysulka, eat I beg of you!" he sobbed. "You will be free this night, my lovely, by all the Gods do I swear it! Only please, please eat, or you'll not have the strength to fly. See! 'Tis fresh and warm, dead for but a moment — eat, Ysulka!"

He laid the dead rat on the block beside the bird and sank gasping and crying into the straw as she tore at the carcass, dipping her beak in again and again, eating ravenously. An hour later Finbar roused himself again to see the alert Gyrfalcon watching him intently. He felt, through his haze of pain and weakness, the now familiar touch of her mind. Without a second thought he reached up for her and she, in return, made no move to resist him.

Under cover of darkness he carried her to the stable-yard, then out beyond the castle walls. Into the woods he staggered carrying his precious burden. When he stumbled to his knees a third time, and could not rise again, he set her down. She was very weak from her ordeal but not so weak that she could not win her freedom! With but a few beats of her magnificent wings she cleared the tree-tops.

Circling once, twice, thrice around the boy she screamed and was gone.

Finbar raised his fist to her in salute, tears coursing from his remaining eye, blood running free from the gaping wound that had been the other, then blackness rushed up to claim him once more.

Finbar did not know if he would live or die . . . "But at least," he thought, "I know, now, the difference!" '

* * *

Take up the consecrated oil and rub the Blade of your Athame with it in honour of the Beings of the Element of Air.

To complete the Ritual you will give thanks to the Lord and Lady of all living. Go to the Gate of Air, firstly, and see the Being standing sentinel there. Have your Athame with you and raise it to the Guardian, and say:

Powers of Air,
Place of Dawn,
Guardian of the Gate
I pledge my Air to thine!
Depart in peace to whence ye came
Until we meet again!

Draw the Banishing Pentagram of Air upon the ether before you, as you have been taught, and watch as the Being mirrors it from his side of the Threshold. See him go, and watch as the Gate closes. Extinguish the Candle with the tip of your Blade.

Proceed to the North. See the Being standing sentinel at the Gate. Raise your Athame in salute, and say:

Powers of Fire,
Place of the Highest Sun,
Guardian of the Gate
I pledge my Fire to thine!
Depart in peace to whence ye came
Until we meet again!

Draw the Banishing Pentagram of Fire on the ether before you and watch as the Being mirrors it from his side of the Threshold. See him go, and watch as the Gate closes. When it is done then extinguish the Candle of the North with the tip of your Blade.

Proceed to the West. See the Being standing sentinel there. Raise your Athame in salute, and say

Powers of Water,
Place of the Setting Sun,

Guardian of the Gate
I pledge my Water to thine!
Depart in peace to whence ye came
Until we meet again!

Draw the Banishing Pentagram of Water on the ether before you
and watch as the Being mirrors it from his side of the Threshold.
See him go, and watch as the Gate closes. Extinguish the Candle
to the West.

Proceed to the South. See the Being standing sentinel. Raise
your Athame in salute, and say:

Powers of Earth,
Place of the Deepest Night,
Guardian of the Gate
I pledge my Earth to thine!
Depart in peace to whence ye came
Until we meet again!

Draw the Banishing Pentagram of Earth on the ether before
you, and watch as the Being mirrors it from his side of the
Threshold. See him go, and watch as the Gate closes. Extinguish
the Candle of the South.

Complete the Circle by continuing until you stand back at the
East. Focus intent and, using your Athame, draw the electric-
blue light of the Circle back into the Blade, and from there
direct it back to the Inner Planes to aid you in the building of
your Inner Temple.

The Rituals of Fire and Water

For the following two Rituals I shall give you the basics
— i.e. the requirements, the place from which to begin your
Ritual, the Legend and the chant for power-raising — and you
are to prepare the rest of these two Rituals from what you have
absorbed thus far, taking care over detail and intent. Having

absorbed the Rituals of Earth and Air you should be able to write the 'seeings' of each Gate-opening for yourself. Just follow the established Pattern of Ritual.

The Ritual of Fire
(*The Alliance of Finias*)
Within your Circle you will require the following:

Ritual Tools
Wand; Athame; Pentacle; Cup; white Cord; Salt and Water; Wine (within your Cup); five candlesticks; five red candles; your Robe if required; Incense; consecrated oil; a red cloth onto which you have either painted or sewn the Hermetic symbol of Fire:

Also your tape of the Inner Voyage, 'The Elemental Dragon of Fire', plus the tape-player; matches to light the candles and Incense; your book and pen for recording the experiences; a head-cloth.

When you and your Temple are in readiness you will cast the Circle in the usual manner, centre yourself and begin the Ritual at the *Gate of Fire*.

The chant to use for the raising of power prior to the Inner Voyage is:

By the Seed beneath the Snow;
By the Fingers of the Flame;
By the Forge, the Power of Shaping;
By Stellar Fire
I bid thee come!

When you have followed the whole Ritual Pattern you will close as usual.

N.B. Remember you are working with Fire of Fire, Water of Fire, Earth of Fire, Air of Fire.

*   *   *

The Legend of the Dragon of Fire

'An untidy sprawl of younglings, clothed in shades of
forest green, and seeming to merge into the very woods that
surrounded them, lay, sat or knelt in a silent study of single-
mindedness, each with a common purpose. So intent were they
upon their task that none seemed at all aware of the green and
golden tranquillity and beauty of their surroundings, nor of the
myriad of dancing, rainbow shards that were the birds and
insects of the grove. They bent as one over their work, in
identical pose of total concentration, quills moving slowly and
deliberately to create a script of perfect grace upon their fine
parchments.

The ancient tomes from which they copied were set
reverently before them, protected from the ground by
exquisitely embroidered cloths, a few to be shared amongst the
many, for precious and rare were they.

Beneath a tree, his back set against its lichened trunk, sat the
aged Elder into whose care these novices were entrusted. He
rose, grumbling and with difficulty, leaning hard upon his Staff
for support, and stooped to peer upon the work of a youngster
caught gazing vacantly, inward looking, unseeing of his
comrades and surroundings.

"Translate!" the old Master said softly, yet with a note in his
voice that commanded instant attention. The dark-haired youth
was brought back from his far-flung reveries with a jolt, yet
spared a brief upward glance and rueful smile before beginning
to translate his work from the ancient script into the common
tongue.

"The Book of Tzu C'aadath Mut," he read, "the Dragon of
the Crystal Flame. This being the eleventh Book of the
Chronicles of Trin-Da'ath. Chapter 1, verse 1: 'There was one
amongst the Dakiti, Warrior Priests of Trin-Da'ath, who was
named Finias. And his Staff was named Khatia, and bound
together were they two through the Will and the Power.' Verse 2:
'Then it came upon Finias to take upon himself a mighty Oath,
and bound by that Oath he'. . . ." the student paused and twisted
around to look up at the proud old man behind him.

"Master," he said quietly, "tell thee the tale, for we would ever hear it from thy lips before the dry old words of Scripture." The others ceased writing and looked up, hopefully and expectantly.

The Elder lifted a grey, winged eyebrow and cuffed the lad gently across one ear. "Thou wouldst endure anything rather than work, even an old man's ramblings!" Yet even as he said so he settled himself amongst them, grey eyes sparkling with pleasure, for a gifted Bard was he. And here is the tale he wove:

"The arid landscape seemed to stretch eternally, not only through physical space but through the weave of time itself. To the lone man, treading soft and wary across the heat-hazed plain, it was as if all his yesterdays had been spent thus, and for all his tomorrows was but the same promised.

He was tall, this man, his spare frame lithe and muscular. Beneath a mass of very dark hair, long and wavy, his face was lean and angular; eyes of a surprising depth of grey gazed steadily and openly, set off strikingly by long dark eyebrows which lifted slightly at their outer edges. His nose was straight and narrow, above a wide, though thin-lipped, mouth. He was customarily clean-shaven, but his chin was now darkened and rough with new growth. It was an extraordinarily expressive face: his smile was like the play of dancing sunlight upon clear, bright water; his frown like the distant, ominous rumble of thunder that darkens the Sun and fills the heart with foreboding. A lightning flash of temper, like a bolt of blue fire, often followed that frown, more quickly repented of than forgiven. In Earth years we could reckon his age at about thirty-five or six. His name was Finias. A Warrior-Priest on a self-sought Vision Quest, was he.

In his right hand he carried a Staff, held as one might hold the soul of one's beloved, reverently, intimately, possessively, and yet at the same time almost heedlessly; a part of his very consciousness, and deeper still than that.

The Staff was the mark of his Calling, and bespoke him for

what he was: one of those who were called the Dakiti, the Warrior-Priests whose very name brought honour and respect. Few were chosen to follow this Calling, chosen not by their Elders but by their own unmistakable talent and 'otherness'. The training in Warrior skills went hand-in-glove with that of the Priesthood, every lesson in each being augmented and deepened by its application to the other. Eventually, as each Dakita approached the final Initiation, the two aspects became inseparable, and neither the Warrior nor the Priest could exist without its otherself. Nor could there be a single impulse, thought or emotion that either one alone could lay claim to.

Finias was one such a man. Trudging now, as he was, across a landscape alien and harsh, he thought long upon these matters, as if to keep alive his awareness of who he was, and what he was. Upon that awareness depended his survival and the success of his Quest. His Staff, which he grasped white-knuckled, caressing the wood with his thumb, was not a weapon yet it was the greatest weapon that he had. It was made of dense, black wood, incredibly old, preserved by a quirk of nature deep in the mysterious Sacred Groves, where none but Dakiti Elders could go. It was said that each Staff lay waiting, dormant and as yet half formed, buried in the boggy ground, to be claimed by the one to whom they were promised. These ancient lengths of wood were living, sentient remains of the Mother Forest, and from the depths of this Forest, so sayeth the Legends, all life did spring. Each Dakiti Initiate spent much time in the Forest Sanctuary that surrounded the Sacred Groves in communion with the Spirit of the Forest; for here was Her Soul. As the final Initiation approached a new Staff would emerge from the black mire in which it had dwelt for millennia. This event, and this alone, was the mark of acceptance of the new Initiate. Thereafter, bonds beyond life itself were forged as each Dakita, attuned to the sentient wood, created a thing of astonishing beauty and power. Suffused with the Magical Will of a fully trained and initiated Warrior-Priest, there was nothing that could command more awe or respect than a Dakiti Staff.

The Quest of Finias was the stuff, as they say, of which legends are made (and would be made, too, in the time yet to come), but legends are notoriously hard in the making and heroes go generally unsung in their hour of greatest need. Finias had undertaken a task of breathtaking audacity, it being no less than to regenerate an ailing Sun.

The wisest Dakiti Elders had known of their Sun's degeneration for many lifetimes, but now the failing light and warmth of the planet's life-sustaining solar Star could be perceived by any of its humblest folk. Through the sacred teachings of his Path, Finias knew that all the possibilities and potentials for his world were ever present in the Intelligence of the manifest Universe. He also knew, and the knowing was sacred and secret, that this Intelligence resided, in the physical realm, within the Holy Caves of Knowledge, at the very heart of the Sacred Groves.

These Caves ran deep, ah! deeper than you can imagine, through the living earth and rock of the planet and beyond. Here dwelt the Mind behind the Mother Forest, the Heart that conceived all Life, and the Will that made it manifest! To enter the Holy Caves was to enter the Intelligence centre of Life Itself. The twisting labyrinths of endless passageways, caverns, pits and high-vaulted ceilings of unimaginable complexity were the very braincells of the Universe. What resided therein was every thought, idea, dream, memory, desire and regret that the Spirit of Being had ever known — and there was also every unmanifest possibility made manifestly possible if one only knew how to harness the enormous power that lay hidden in the Caves.

Finias did *not* know. He only knew that the Caves contained such Power, though true understanding of the phenomenon eluded him, as indeed it must elude any mortal mind. What he lacked in understanding, however, Finias made up for in faith, courage and imagination, and thusly armed did he set forth upon his Quest.

Once he had stepped within the first of the Holy Caves (after taking leave of the Elders, gathered in Ritual and deep in trance to aid him), Finias learned quickly that the mouth of each Cave was the Threshold into Elsewhere; entire worlds lay within each new Cave, some unspeakably beautiful, others unimaginably terrible. Some Caves seemed to draw him in, tugging at him physically as they beguiled him emotionally. Others repelled him, some quite viciously, or sadly, or angrily. Everywhere Finias felt the constant passing of energy current, darting and flowing around or through him. Eventually he felt these impulses of energy actually guiding him, leading him on through a twisted, improbable route that brought him at last before a Cave, brilliantly lit from within.

The world upon which he gazed was bathed in clear, hot, golden light. A huge Sun hung high at its zenith, radiating heat and power into a shimmering noon sky. A flat plain stretched before him, climbing steeply at the horizon towards massive outcrops of rock. Beyond these a mountain stood, the top of which was blown clean away. A wisp of dark smoke issued forth from within its ruined peak. The roar of lions could be heard from a distance, and a golden eagle spiralled slowly above the plain. Sparkling and winking from somewhere within the massed boulders of the rocky outcrop a shining brilliance caught the watcher's eye, and Finias stepped forward into this land of Elsewhere.

He was watched, this man, as he made his lonely way across the dry plain, where time behaved not as he felt it ought and the Sun hung motionless in a white-hot sky. There was One who dwelt within a lair hidden amongst the rocks; One whose great age defied imagining; One whose wisdom spanned the comings and goings of whole worlds; One who remembered such things as the very Gods had forgotten: Tzu C'aadath Mut, Dragon of the Crystal Flame.

The Dragon watched Finias' approach with a patience made endless by the slow trundle of aeons passing by. Through heavily lidded eyes, seeming yet to doze and dream, he watched the man's perseverance that brought him closer and yet closer to the Cave that was Dragon-Lair. Into this Cave there was but one way, that being also the only way out, and it was guarded by the beast's be-fanged and sulphurous snout. The approach to the Crystal's Cave, for that is what it was, climbed steeply up a narrow path — more a fragile flight of steps of loosely held shards of rock. The climb itself began from deep within a ravine. At the bottom of the ravine lay . . . ah, but I run ahead of my tale! Let us walk again with Finias awhile and see through his eyes what wonders this place might hold.

Time, as I have before mentioned, seemed not to exist in this place in any way that Finias could reckon, and was only measured by the increased weariness of body and mesmerisation of the mind. Distance, on the other hand, appeared to be entirely subjective, and by constant application of concentration and focus of intent, Finias found the smoking volcano towards which he was headed could be brought closer to him, or at least fixed in an otherwise shifting landscape. Concentrated Will was the only antidote to the poison of doubt and uncertainty that this unreliable world leeched into his veins.

Pausing but infrequently to rest in the shade of the sparse, scrubby vegetation, Finias strode, trance-like, towards his goal. Before him radiant, multi-hued splinters of brilliant light glittered tantalizingly from within the rocks, drawing him on. Suddenly the plain came to an abrupt and complete end, dropping down an almost sheer cliff-face into a deep ravine before climbing again, just as steeply, up to the volcano's side. Blistering heat seared the air even to the height upon which Finias now stood, aghast and dismayed — for along the bottom of the ravine, about a half a mile straight down, ran a tortuous river of molten lava.

Clutching his precious Staff desperately in his hands he knelt upon the stony ground and pressed his forehead wearily against the wood. 'Oh . . . Gods!' he whispered. His answer was a deep, booming chuckle that rolled and echoed around the massive rocks and boulders on the other side of the narrow gorge. He jerked his head up and stared intently towards the chaotic tumble of caves and ledges, pinnacles and clefts that was the rock face before him. What he saw made his eyes widen and his breath a long, indrawn hiss.

The Dragon was green and gold and red, red, red, each colour translucent and shimmering over lapping, metallic scales. Larger than the biggest Gathering Hall Finias had ever seen, the creature shifted slowly to emerge partially from its cave, swinging its enormous head from side to side upon a serpentine, scaly neck. Curved yellow fangs protruded downwards from its jaws and smoke trickled forth from flared nostrils. Set wide upon the knobby head, bright green eyes glinted in the hot sunlight — and the thing was, quite unmistakably, laughing. 'A thousand welcomes, friend Finias,' said a deep, rich voice, coming somehow not through the air but into Finias' mind, 'disturber of my peace and trespasser upon my lands, why come you here?'

Finias drew a deep breath in order to shout his answer across the gulf that (thankfully) separated him from the mighty beast, but upon reflection he, too, spoke in his mind. 'O Great One,' he said with a stiff bow, for bowing came not easily to Finias, 'I come upon a Quest born of dire need, for the help of my people and our benighted world. I sought not to disturb your Eminence, nor in any way challenge or thwart you.'

'That,' replied the Dragon, 'is what they *all* say!' and he laughed again.

'If I could but explain . . .' Finias tried again, but the Dragon cut him off mid-sentence.

'Explain? Explain yourself to me? You fool of a man! Do you not think that I might *know* of all your explanations even before you form them in your mind? Everything that you do know is but a fragment of my greater knowledge! Every thought and dream and memory of yours is held somewhere in the treasury of *my* mind if I should care to look and seek it out! Look! See for yourself!' and into Finias' consciousness the Dragon projected a rapid sequence of images and emotions — scenes from his childhood, memories long faded yet painfully poignant when awakened. The long, long hours of study and training, some of tedium and dry rote learning, and others of breathless excitement and discovery were re-lived in an instant. Moments of joy and pride and ecstasy were mingled bewilderingly with memories of pain and loss and shame. Successes and failures flitted across his mind as Finias fought to keep his sanity against the onslaught, hopes and dreams and most secret longings tumbled one upon the other, drawing him down and down. Then suddenly it all stopped, save that *she* was there, loosed from the deepest part of his hidden self where he had locked her away years ago. He looked again upon that memory which he had vowed he would see no more; the deep red hair framing a pale, pointed face; eyes of hazel-green, wide and all-knowing; her body supple, willow-thin, leaning towards him as her fine boned hands held themselves palms upwards, towards him. Her lips parted and she spoke his name, softly, imploringly.

Finias screamed, 'No-o-o! Damn you! Damn you! Fuck you!' He screamed himself hoarse at the unmoving Dragon until, totally spent, he sank sobbing to the ground and pressed his face against the hot, stony earth. He rose, shakily, some moments later, leaning heavily upon his Staff.

'*Friend* Dragon,' he said with bitter emphasis, 'since it would seem that you do, indeed, know all of me, then my Quest is no mystery to you. And neither, I would guess, is the answer for which I seek. What brought me to this place?' The Dragon made no reply but moved a little to one side of his cave. Immediately a blinding flash of rainbow light burst forth from behind the Dragon, causing Finias to shield his eyes, and lighting the land around with brilliant splashes of colour. Squinting against the almost painful radiance Finias perceived a huge, multi-faceted Crystal standing upon a ledge of quartz within the Dragon's cave.

The light from the Crystal came from within itself, its centre like molten Fire. The Dragon spoke softly, reverently: 'The Crystal Flame, friend Finias! The Heart and Soul of Fire itself! And yours, my friend, yours for the taking.'

This seemed highly improbable to Finias and he had not expected his Quest to be an easy one, nor yet to have answers given freely, without cost. Suspiciously he asked, scrutinising the impossible ravine with its deadly river below, 'How do I come to you?'

The Dragon bent his head downwards to survey the molten inferno between them. 'You walk,' replied the Dragon casually.

'Yeah,' thought Finias, 'that figures!'

105

Once having left the height at the end of the plain behind him Finias found that the descent was disconcertingly easy. The steepness of the sides made normal walking, or even climbing, an impossibility, and by the time he had finished slithering and scraping down the rough volcanic rock he had left much of his leathern clothing, and not a little of his own hide, behind him. He tumbled to the bottom of the ravine, still thankfully some several yards away from the river of molten fire. He was bruised and raw and in a very bad mood. The Dragon had lumbered forth from the mouth of his cave and sat atop the opposite cliff with his head hanging down its side, watching Finias' descent.

'Very elegant,' he said softly and sarcastically into Finias' mind. Finias forebore to reply. The heat from the lava flow blistered his skin, stung his eyes and seared his lungs with every breath. It was not, however, as intense as he had feared, the gorge acting as a natural funnel to draw much of the hot air upwards and outwards away from its source. The man squatted where he had landed, sitting on his heels, and went deep into meditation, laying his Staff, which had naturally never left his grasp, across his knees.

'Ground and centre . . .' he murmured to himself, recalling the earliest of his trainings, 'breathe . . . ground . . . centre.' He sought from within his Soul the spark of his own Spiritual Fire, sought it as a physical reality, a Violet Flame burning softly and steadily at his own self's heart. He found that which he sought and embraced it eagerly, thankfully: a bright, clear Flame that he recognised, knew and loved! He spoke his Magical Name into the Flame — 'Tu El Shirron, Tu El Shirron'. The Flame leapt and grew, joyfully. Finias fed it, as one would feed a physical Fire, and the fuel he offered into its burning heart was the very stuff of which his life itself was made. His every Truth and his very Faith he called forth and sacrificed it to that Fire. His memories and longings, dreams and long-cherished hopes (some of which had lain long dormant before the Great Dragon had awakened them in him) he took, one by one, and watched them as they took flame and burned. Less and less of the man was there, and more and more of the wild, free Fire — until at last there was only that one last memory, a pain beyond bearing, a loss for which he had never known comfort, a wound that would never heal. He methodically brought forth every detail of her face, the lilt of her voice, the feel of her body against his. The times of joy, of peace, of ecstasy; the times of fierce quarrelling, of grief and reconciliation; the laughter and the tears. He recalled the anguish he suffered, unreasonably protective, as she struggled with the arduous Dakiti training, and the joy he knew when he was present at her final Initiation.

And heedless of the sobs that rent his Soul he relived the anguish of her passing, on a perilous Quest, in an alien land where he could not reach her. He breathed her Name brokenly into his Spirit Fire — 'Hakashi, Hakashi', and the Flame leapt wildly, and consumed him utterly.

Finias stood and walked to the edge of the molten river. He stepped forward into that liquid Fire and he walked.

The oozing, crusted lava gave at his footfall, and he walked. The sluggish Flames licked at his ankles and his calves, and he walked. The incredible heat boiled and lapped about his flesh, and he walked. His Staff glowed red-hot in his clenched hand and the clothes he wore blistered and blackened upon his skin — and he walked. He walked across the lava bed until he reached the other side, and he paused not once, not even to wonder at it. Then he climbed, and he climbed until he stood before the entrance to the Cave of the Crystal where the Great Dragon waited, watching him in silence — and in awe, and in love.

'I come for what is mine,' said Finias aloud, his ringing tone echoing around the vast Cave.

'Indeed,' Tzu C'aadath Mut replied softly, 'it is yours.'

The colossal beast swung aside, cramped against the wall of his Cave, as Finias moved towards the huge, brilliant Star of a Crystal. As he reached out his hand slowly, tentatively, to touch it, the Cave became filled with a symphony of harmonious sound, peal upon peal of exquisite tone, emanating from the Crystal itself.

As Finias looked deeply into the Crystal's fiery depths he saw *her* face gazing back at him. She looked older, wiser, and her eyes were filled with a great gentleness. There was pride and awe there too, as she smiled at him. Then the vision faded and Finias made ready to leave. Wrapping the Crystal in the tattered remains of his cloak, he bound it in what was left of the leather thonging that had strapped his now non-existent leggings to his calves. Fastening his precious burden to his back he turned and began to walk out of the Cave.

He looked to neither left nor right, seeing, yet unseeing, only straight ahead. As he reached the mouth of the Cave the Dragon spoke a final time: 'Leave me not,' he said. Finias paused but did not turn. 'Finias,' the voice persisted, 'look at me.' The man's back was rigid, tensed and still. Slowly, reluctantly, he turned his head until his eyes met those brilliant green orbs.

'Can it be that still you know me not?' There was pain in the Dragon's voice. 'I am but your own Self, Finias. You created me between you, you and she, and here have I dwelt since before the Dawn of Time, waiting for you to claim me.' The Dragon's form shimmered and wavered in the hot air as Finias watched, then he felt his body shift, sickeningly, as Tzu C'aadath Mut possessed him, then he the Dragon.

The age and the wisdom, the Power and Life, he took it all. The Cave of the Crystal he knew then to be yet another within the Holy Caves of Knowledge where his journey had begun. Moreover, he knew the way home. Bearing his precious gift, the Crystal Flame, that held the Spirit of Fire, he returned to his own realm where the Sun in his own sky awaited its regeneration. The Quest of Finias was ended."

The white-haired Elder, his tale finished and made stronger in the re-weaving, was silent and unmoving, save for the running tears that he wept. The students, noiseless, moved as one to gather quills, parchments and books, and crept softly from his presence. Each paused, involuntarily, before leaving the Sacred Grove to turn and gaze with renewed awe upon the Great Crystal, glowing and humming upon its Altar.'

* * *

108

The Ritual of Water
(*The Alliance of Murias*)
Within your Circle you will require the following:

Ritual Tools
Cup; Athame; Wand; Pentacle; white Cord; Salt; Water (within your Cup); five candlesticks; five deep-blue candles; your Robe if required; Incense; consecrated oil; a deep-blue cloth onto which you will have either painted or sewn the Hermetic symbol of Water:

Also your tape of the Inner Voyage, 'The Elemental Fish of Water', plus the tape-player; matches to light the candles and Incense; your book and pen for recording your experience; a head-cloth.

When you and your Temple are in readiness you will cast your Circle, centre yourself and begin the Ritual at the *Gate of Water*.

The chant to use for the raising of power prior to the Inner Plane Voyage is:

By the Queen of Ancient Magic!
By the Rainbow in the Storm!
By the Lake, The Isle Remembered!
By Sea of Space
I bid thee come!

When you have followed the whole Ritual Pattern you will close as usual.

*   *   *

The Legend of the Fish of Water
'When the man's horse could run no more he allowed her to slow to a trot, then to a walk, then he reined her to a halt. He dismounted and left her where she stood, her head

drooping and her eyes glazed with exhaustion. To simply walk on and leave his horse thus, without the gentle, generous care to which she was accustomed, was unthinkable. Collum did it; partly because he had given up thinking several hours ago, in the midst of battle, and also because just a short half-day ago he had committed such an act of outrage against the very fibre of his soul that walking away from his distressed horse seemed negligible by comparison.

The sun would soon set and the man cast about in his empty mind to seek out the reason why this should seem so significant. Ah! Yes! With the setting sun came darkness, cold and danger; perhaps even death, though Collum doubted that he would be that fortunate. The horse raised her head and blew softly through her nose as she watched him walk away from her, her laboured breathing making even the snort barely possible; she dragged a hoof forward in a feeble attempt to follow, but the step became a stumble. Sinking to her knees she despairingly allowed the rest of her body to follow, and lay gasping and foaming at the mouth, her eyes fixed and staring, at the man's receding back.

Before Collum lay a grey, mist-shrouded lake stretching widely to either side. In the descending gloom the distance between him and the Water was hard to judge, but his feet, seemingly drawn to it by a will of their own, measured neither time nor distance as they doggedly pressed on, one before the other.

On the far horizons, to the left and right of the lake, grew the autumn-decked trees of the forest, stretching around the waters like encircling arms to disappear into the mists that hid the distant shore. The open, flat land across which the man walked sloped imperceptibly down towards the water, becoming marshier and boggier as he came closer to the lake.

There was an occasional hillock, covered with sparse, hardy grasses, over which the man climbed, not having sufficient presence of mind to save himself the effort by going round. He reached the edge of the lake as the last light faded from the sky, and the worst day in Collum's life ended. He knelt at the water's edge to drink and splash his face and neck, then wrapping himself within his cloak, he leant back against a rock and wept.

From a small rise within the lake a figure stood watching. If seen from the shore she would have appeared to be wreathed in mist, drops of water glistening in her damp hair, her breath frosting slightly before her face. From where she stood, however, the ground beneath her feet was green and firm, the sky above her head was clear and tinged with the glorious hues of Sunset, the lapping waters of the lake were blue and silver and sparkled in the clean air around her. There was no mist where she stood, yet the man on the shore was seen as though through a vaporous, shifting veil, as her gaze fell upon him.

The woman, whose heart was touched by the sight of Collum's grief and despair, was tall and dark. Her long hair lay smoothed away from her brow and was loosely bound at intervals with bands of soft, white cloth as it fell to below her hips. Her gown was also white, girdled with silver. She had a dove-grey, woollen cloak around her shoulders, the deep cowl thrown back. At her waist hung a small, black-handled knife, and around her throat lay a silver chain upon which hung a delicately wrought Crescent Moon. She was young, perhaps sixteen or seventeen years, and seemed hesitant and uncertain as she observed the man upon the shore.

Casting several glances around her, a worried frown between her brows, she seemed suddenly to become resolved. Raising her white-skinned arms above her head, the long delicately fingered hands moving briefly in an exquisitely lyrical gesture, she spoke. Her musical voice filled the air for but an instant, seemingly accompanied by the faraway chiming of a high-toned bell . . . the scene around her shimmered and vanished. She stepped forward into the mist . . .

Collum had watched his son die that afternoon. In the midst of a battle that had little to distinguish it from the many others he had fought, Collum had seen Rev go down, and in that instant he not only lost his son but the fabric of his life was torn apart.

Even though Collum was a passionate, creative man, his thoughts, values and even his emotions were prescribed by his cultural heritage. There was no room for innovative or anarchistic behaviour amongst Collum's people, and each action and response, no matter how deeply felt, followed a time-honoured, invariable formula.

When Collum had watched as his son's body was trampled into the bloody, muddy ground, he had expected to be stirred to even greater effort and fury. He should have fought like a man possessed, making sure to take the head of the warrior who had slain his son. Later that night he would have delivered an impassioned eulogy for Rev before his feasting, victorious clan.

What had actually happened to Collum as he witnessed his son's death was as incomprehensible to him as it would have been to any other member of his tribe. The sights and sounds of the battle had faded before his eyes and he saw instead, as if through a fine mist, a tiny red-headed baby held proudly in his young mother's arms. He watched Rev's first tottering steps on sturdy little legs, and heard again the first time the child had spoken his name.

Again and again, one after the other, scenes from his son's childhood rolled past his eyes and he felt rising, as if from the ground and up through his body, a flow of love and grief so mighty he knew his soul to be swept away by it. Rather than hatred his soul ached with tenderness as he looked around with new eyes. In every face, be it friend or foe, he saw a son or a daughter, a mother, father, brother, sister or friend. He saw, in every rage-contorted face, someone he wanted to reach out to, to hold and keep safe, a person with whom he could share life and laughter.

Quite suddenly he was a stranger in an alien, incomprehensible world of hatred, violence and bloodshed . . . and he simply dropped his sword and walked away.

The single-minded warriors around him were conditioned to respond to aggression and attack; it was not honour that prevented them from cutting down an unarmed man, they simply did not see him. He found his horse, mounted, turned her head away from the battle, away from home, and rode.

Then, when she could run no more, he walked alone . . . and here he sat, at the edge of the mist-covered, unfamiliar lake, at Sunset. As alone as only a man who has stepped out of his whole reality can be.

Collum's gloomy prediction proved to be correct: he did not die in the night. Of course, there had been no reason why he should, yet he faced the day as one not wholly alive. True, his body screamed of its mortality with every chilled, stiff movement, the damp and cold practically immobilising him — but his mind and his heart, perhaps his very soul, lay unresponsive beneath a shroud of fear, grief and loneliness. Even the early sunshine of the autumn day, dawning warm and clear as Collum woke, did not dispel the white mists which swirled and eddied above the water of the lake.

The white-robed woman who had walked across hidden raised paths that criss-crossed the lake paused a little way from the edge and stood gravely watching as Collum rose. He started visibly as he noticed her standing motionless among the mists, seeming to stand upon the water itself.

"Woman," he whispered, "if woman ye be, what is this place? What lies yonder amongst this unearthly mist?" The woman turned, smiling. As she took a step away from him she turned her head to look over her shoulder.

"Follow me", she said softly, "and find out!" Collum felt that he had nothing left to lose; having been raised to accept the supernatural as just another part of the whole order of things, the fact that he intuitively sensed an "otherworldliness" about the lake, the mist and the woman did not daunt him. He followed the disappearing woman, finding no difficulty in perceiving the hidden pathways through the water once he stepped forth. The sunlight filtered down through the white mists, creating a pale, golden glow above the mirrored surface. Water-fowl, fish, frogs and insects abounded in the moist environment, lending more of an air of normality to the place.

Eventually the dark-haired woman paused and held out a hand towards him. He stopped, but did not respond to her gesture. "There are rivers here," she said, "that rush boldly to the sea from their mountain home. There are towering falls over which the waters tumble wildly . . ."

"In a *lake*?" cried the man incredulously. The woman smiled and shrugged.

"The mighty Salmon swims here," she continued, "Fighting his way back to his birthplace. Find him and catch him, Collum, for he alone can help you."

"A fish," said Collum flatly. "You tell me to wander around in a lake searching for a fish that swims up rivers and waterfalls — *also* in a lake — because it can help me?"

"Do you have anything better to do?" she asked. Collum did not answer, as the woman turned and walked away into the mists.

For the rest of that day, and the next, and the next, he wandered alone through the strange, boggy world of mist and water, marvelling at the wonders hidden within. Rivers, he did indeed find, and small islands covered in trees rising up from the water. In such a place thirst was not a problem, but food was hard to come by. He found watercress growing amongst the rocks in abundance, but it was hardly sustaining fare. Eventually he resorted to catching fish, and once a bird, and succeeded in partially cooking them over a fitful fire made from damp wood on one of those islands. He felt uncomfortable throughout this whole process, however, having a vague sense of disquiet as he took the creatures' lives within the eerie silence of the strange world through which he wandered.

On the third night as he prepared to sleep before another damp, smoky fire, the woman appeared again. As his loneliness had begun to oppress him and he found his memories sad company, his heart lifted at the sight of her as she materialised out of the mist in front of him. She was dressed as before, but this time her cloak was wrapped closely around her and her head was hidden within the deep folds of the hood.

"It was cold in my world," she said, as she pushed the hood back from her face. Her words mystified Collum, but his thoughts did not dwell upon them. Indeed, Collum's thoughts had lain dormant for the past three days and nights; nothing surprised him, nothing troubled him. He was living from moment to moment, obeying his instincts and following his intuition. Of thoughts he had none, but of feelings he had a surfeit. It seemed to Collum that within his breast there raged a storm of emotion. Every sight, sound and smell he encountered evoked an emotional response. He responded to the mystical world through which he journeyed with a bewildering mixture of wonder, delight, fear, sadness and joy. Completely missing from his experiences were hatred, anger and aggression. Whilst these had once formed a cornerstone of his life, now they became as elusive as a bad dream, not quite remembered.

The young woman seated herself before his fire and stretched out her hands towards the struggling flame. Shivering, she gazed intently at the fire and spoke a few words under her breath. Collum heard a faint rushing sound within his head, then jumped as the fire crackled and sprang to new life, eagerly consuming the wood.

"Ah, that's better," the woman seemed to speak to herself. She raised her eyes to Collum's and smiled. "I could not stay away," she said, "I can feel your every movement as you wander within this place. Sometimes the scrying bowl shows me where you are and how you fare. Our Holy Mother keeps close watch over you and communes silently with our Goddess Danu to divine the meaning of your coming. She, too, must bide her time until you are ready to come into our world." She sighed. "Few men come now to the Holy Isle, and of those, fewer still remain. Oh, it's true we need Initiates to go abroad into the world to keep the Word of the Goddess alive in the hearts of men, but much more do we need the men who *know* Her to dwell amongst us in Her service. The Goddess, like Her Priestesses, grows weary of only female company, I fear."

There was a pause while she seemed absorbed in her thoughts, then suddenly she rose in a quick, fluid movement and, laughing, cast off her cloak.

"Collum," she cried, "I will dance for you!" and dance she did. With stamping feet and clapping hands, her head, shoulders and hips weaving a sensuous pattern as she moved with ever-quickening steps around and around the fire. Her eyes flashed and her hair spun around her to the sounds of her bracelets and armbands tinkling and jangling in rhythm. Collum watched entranced, his heart yearning for her as she whirled and weaved in the firelight. The silver Crescent at her throat caught the glow of the flames and shone like the Moon Herself. Everything about her bemused and fascinated Collum, so strange and exotic did it all seem, yet, at the same time, hauntingly familiar. She finished her dance gasping and laughing, then raised her arms, spoke, and was gone.

"Noooo!!" cried Collum, reaching out to the space where she had stood. He fell forward, pressing his face to the ground where she had stood. Hot tears muddied the ground beneath his face. Long, long did he weep.

Morning found him journeying on, the pain he had felt at the girl's disappearance now a dull, raw ache sitting like a stone in his chest. He was almost upon the waterfall before he realised it, the thunderous noise eventually piercing his consciousness as he wandered dazedly.

He stopped and gazed wonderingly at the magnificent sight before him. The towering majesty of huge rocks rose high above him; the broiling white water that leaped and danced over them and the deep green pool, surprisingly still, at the base of the falls, astounded his incredulous eyes . . and there, at the base of the falls, swam the largest Salmon that Collum had ever seen, leaping and writhing with enormous effort and strength. The huge fish was obviously striving to leap the falls. Each mighty effort took it at least halfway up the rocks before it fell back again with a great splash. Collum remembered the woman's words: "Find him and catch him, Collum, for he alone can help you!"

A moment's observation was all Collum needed to see that catching the Salmon would not be difficult. It seemed never to leap quite high enough to clear the falls, and every effort must surely sap its strength. Collum sat by the edge of the pool, and waited.

Eventually, inevitably, the fish lay still in the pool, gills heaving as it strove for watery breath, its eyes fixed sorrowfully upon the top of the waterfall. Without warning Collum leapt into the water, grasping with both brawny arms the huge Salmon and hauling it, struggling, to the bank. Even in its exhausted state the fish put up a good fight, until, eventually, both Collum and the Salmon lay sprawled upon the grass.

"So," spoke the fish in a deep, rich voice, "my Doom is upon me. And thou art the instrument of my Destiny. Make haste, my son, make haste!"

Collum was totally mystified. "What would you have me do?" he asked.

"The decision is thine," replied the fish, "and always has been. As thou canst see I am a fish out of water, and soon, therefore, to die. Thou, too, hast been a fish out of water in thine own world, and the pain of it hast nearly killed thee! Shall we cast ourselves together, thee and I, Collum, upon the waters of life that flow from the Womb and return to the Womb? Have faith and I will take thee home!"

With a mighty heave the fish leapt back into the pool. Without thinking Collum followed. Instantly he regretted it. The pool was dark and cold and deep, and Collum could not swim! He sank into the murky depths, swallowing and breathing water. He almost surrendered to the blackness threatening to engulf him when he again saw the Salmon swimming before him. With a quick flick of its tail it was gone, and Collum instinctively followed.

Now, at the base of the waterfall swam not one, but two Salmon! Together, side by side, moving as one, they leapt once, twice and thrice, their enormous thrusts taking them incredibly upwards, through the great press of water bearing down on them, to emerge at the top of the falls. A few more flicks of mighty tail and fin and they gained the sanctuary of a small backwater.

The Salmon lay motionless in the warm sun, recovering its strength, as the man dragged himself, heaving and gagging, to the bank. He lay there for a long time before being able to discern the change in his surroundings.

The mist was gone, as was the boggy, brackish marshland with its growth of harsh, sour grasses. The ground beneath him was soft and green, covered in lush, deep grass. Around him the air was fresh and dry, bathed in golden sunlight. Above him the sky shone blue and clear, filled with soft breezes and birdsong. He heard a woman's voice.

"So, Morgananu, *this* is your man? He is old, I fear, to train for the Priesthood; think you, truly, that this is the reason for his Quest?"

"So speaks the Goddess in my heart," replied another, familiar, voice. Collum's heart leapt in his breast.

"He is a one such as we need," the voice continued, "a man who knows his own manhood, and still chooses love over hatred and life over death. He has walked the mists and swum with the Salmon!" The dark-haired young woman knelt beside Collum, her eyes smiling into his. She laid her hand upon his arm and raised her face to her High Priestess.

"Holy Mother, the Goddess Herself has chosen this man. Many others also has She chosen but they close their ears and hearts to Her. This man chose to listen. Let us will that he is the first of many, and prepare ourselves for an end to our long, lonely wait."'

* * *

The Solar/Earth Wheel

Rituals of Solstice and Equinox

The Solstice and Equinoctial processions are Ritually acknowledged to align you with these cycles, both personally and environmentally. The mythological symbolism is most important in Ritual context as it allows you to personalise with the cycle and see it as other than 'out there', 'something that just happens', and as such is considered as a process and progression of personal Initiation that aligns you with your Magical Self, the Inner Temple built on the Sacred Four, that spirals you out to dance with the progressions of the Earth around Her Galactic Lover (the Sun). Your Magical Inheritance is irrevocably bound up and interwoven with these progressions, and will allow you to See that the Galaxy dwells within each individual ad infinitum (how to keep your feet on the ground whilst allowing your head to roam amongst the stars!).

It is also important to understand, on an external basis, that our planet, supporting as she does the myriad of diverse lifeforms, *must* be understood. She is not just a piece of dirt to be exploited for her wealth, most of which, when left alone, creates a profound balance that we, at this stage of our conscious development, can only partially comprehend. How much more honourable is it to be, at the very least, careful?

The opening of the self to the Evolving Whole allows you to flow more freely with your own Destiny. It allows you to work at achievement by following the flow of the pattern instead of through personal insistence (i.e. 'working' for expansion in a waning cycle is not always positive or possible; 'working' on inner faculties and detailed learning is enhanced during a waning cycle).

The Solar/Earth progressions begin with the Winter Solstice

(the first stage of the waxing year) and continue around through Spring Equinox, Summer Solstice (the first stage of the waning year) to Autumn Equinox. Interwoven with these are the Fire Festivals of Samhain, Feast of Bride, Beltaen, Llughnassad (but these are not your concern here).

Keys
N.B. Dates given are approximate. Check an Ephemeris for the precise time, annually.

Winter Solstice (22nd June; 22nd December in the northern lands)
Symbolism 'Rebirth of the Sun God. The Boyhood and Training of the Once and Future King.'

Spring Equinox (21st September; 21st March, northern lands)
Symbolism 'Symbolic and Actual Mating of the Sun King with the Daughter of the Moon. His Initiation as Priest and King.'

Summer Solstice (22nd December; 22nd June, northern lands)
Symbolism 'Sacrifice of the Sun King, leading to the Harvest of His Reign: Transformation.'

Autumn Equinox (21st March; 21st September, northern lands)
Symbolism 'Descent through the Realms of Annwn. Power from the Dark Lord to the Virgin Queen of Initiation.'

Notes
The Sabbats are performed as an 'opening' of the cyclic process of the Solar/Earth Wheel. Meditation on the *continuum* is necessary to perceive the Whole; they are not four separate and independent Rituals, merely a point of acknowledgement within the entire and continuous revolution.

At all times it is necessary to recognise that the 'seasons' are internal (Annwn), as well as environmental (Abred), as well as inter-dimensional (Gwynvyd), as well as galactic/universal (Ceugant).

Requirements for the Rituals

Your Altar; your Ritual Tools (4); four point-candles, plus one for the Altar Candle; Salt and Water; Wine and cakes; consecrated Oil of Storax, Amber, Oakmoss; Incense of Sandalwood, Oakmoss resin or oil, Myrrh, oil of nightqueen; the Brazier; your Robe; your Staff; grains and fruit for the Altar; tape-player and tape of the Legend; book and pen for recording your experiences; matches; a head-cloth.

Gather woodchips, etc., prior to the Ritual.

We will summon the Archangelic Lords of the Elements for this Ritual.

The Pattern

Within this story the symbolic relationship between Myth, Magic and the Revolutions of the Solar/Earth Wheel are displayed.

'Without Time, as within Time, there exists a lineage as old as Time — the lineage is the Merlyn and the lineage is the Morgan; the Force of the Wise both male and female, who are of the Great Sea, which is Space.

The Force of the Merlyn is summoned to within the Form of the Wisest of Men; the Force of the Morgan is summoned to within the Form of the Wisest of Women. The Wise Men walk alone but the Wise Women seek each other out and work together; but They know each other always.

Of the Four Fire Festivals, we all know. Of the four the Wisest is the Queen who wears the Crown of Morgan Whose presence is felt at the Time of Samhain. She never quite dwells outside of the Mists but Her Form is seen in the Priestesses of the Moon, both upon the Island and within the World-of-Known.
Now . . .
Know the Legend! For if the Legend dies so does the Magic. Magic is the Gate-Between-the-Worlds and the Gate must be kept open.
So . . .
Understand the above and listen, with mind and heart, to the Legend.

121

In the Caves beneath the World there exist many things, like Dragons and Merlyns and sleeping Kings. To awaken the latter we must summon the former — the Power of the Sacred Seed! The Sacred Seed is implanted within the Womb of an Ancient Queen who does not age, nor lose Her ability to bear fruit. Her representative in time is a Priestess of the Moon who is not known, not acknowledged within the World of Men. She bears the Dragon through the Darkness and to the Daughters of the Moon is born a Son: He-Who-Will-Be-King.

He is taught, by the Merlyn, many things.

He is taught to See, to Walk, to Listen, to Remember, to Learn for Himself. He is taught to Talk, to honour all things of the Sacred, to defend Himself. He is taught the Power of defending more than Himself. He is taught the Speech of Air, of Fire, of Water, of Earth, and He is taught to *do* with what He learns! He learns the Sacred Places. He is given to understand the Instruments of Magic and how they are wielded. He learns about Beauty. He learns about Pain. He is taught Compassion and also Justice. He is taught to Question and to seek the Truth in all things.

He is given the Power to open the Gates-Between-the-Worlds and to Know which is which!

Not much more than a boy is He . . . but He is ready.

He comes to the Island-Outside-of-Time, the Sacred Place that is known to all who tread the Path of Magic, at the Time of Spring.

The Daughters of the Moon choose one from those amongst them. The Force of Morgan is summoned and is invoked within Her by all of them, but especially by the Wisest of Women, Queen of the Lake.

The Boy must prove Himself to the Daughters of the Moon; the Rite of Manhood sees Him running with the Wild to seek His crown. The Lady Morgan awaits Him and sends Him Her strength. He *takes* the Crown.

The Lady Morgan anoints His body with perfumed oils and together they enter the Bower of Flowers that has been prepared for them.

"As the Cup is to Woman so Athame is to Man and co-joined they bring Blessedness!"

With the Dawn they come, loving each other and the One-Who-is-Yet-to-Be.

The Queen of the Lake hands Him the Sword, most Sacred of the Sacred Four, yet in its blood-red Scabbard, and says to Him: "One is nothing without the Other — Justice and Compassion is the Law of the Sword."

And He returns to the World-Within-Time to defend the Places of the World and to fulfil His Time.

He grows Strong in Truth and His Power is known throughout the Land and the People sing His praises for the Earth bears Fruit.

But the Wheel spins and spins and His Fruitfulness is replaced with the Wisdom of Age — and He knows His stay within Time has run its course — the Harvest begins!

His Life is scattered throughout the Fields; He is corn and oats and wheat and barley and apples and all the fruit and grain of the Times.

And His remains are deep within the Earth and the Land lies waiting the Child-of-Promise.

And it all begins again.

And again . . .

And again . . .'

Two things might be of interest to you in preparing to work the Solar Wheel. Firstly, if it is possible, you would greatly enhance the feeling of Festival and Celebration if you had others with you with whom to work — likeminded others. Secondly, if you have the outdoors to hand and can perform the Rituals in the open, then you can have a Staff, other than the one with which you will have consecrated for personal use, for each of the Four Festivals. These can be 'dressed' to suit your creative desires: with bells and/or feathers, leather-work or paints, oils, dyes. Each Staff can then be consecrated at each Ritual and 'planted' at the appropriate Solstice or Equinoctial point of an outdoor Circle in permanent honour of your chosen Path.

Ritual of Winter Solstice

(appropriate time to work: Midnight)

Set up your Temple in the usual manner and bathe with intent of purification.

When you are ready you will seat yourself before the Altar, light the Altar Candle and the Incense, and centre yourself by using four-fold breathing leading to a soft humming chant.

Use your Staff to cast a Circle about yourself, saying:

O Place of Power,
Outside of Time!
Keep all within and all without
And forge a barrier between the two!
I seek the Place beyond the Veil:
O Spear of Light I summon thee
In the Names of the Lady and Lord of All Life!
By Earth, By Sky, By Sea!
So mote it be!

Return to your Altar and take up the Salt in its container and deposit it onto your Pentacle. Place the tip of your Athame Blade within it, and say:

Blessings be upon thee,
Symbol of Earth
Forced from the Womb of the Mother
By the Might of the Sacred Sun!

Draw down the blue light from your Blade and infuse the Salt with it. When this is done replace the Pentacle and Salt upon the Altar and take up the container of Water. Place the tip of your Athame Blade within it, and say:

Out of thee, Water creature,

Goes all that is not Pure!
May only the Essence of the Great Mother remain!

Now add the Salt to the Water and stir the two together. Begin, at the southern-most point of your Circle (North in the northern lands), and sprinkle the boundary of your Circle with the consecrated Water. When this is done then return the container to the Altar. Go to the East with your Censer and cense the Circle with the Incense, then return the Censer to the Altar. Take up the Altar Candle and, beginning at the North (South in the northern lands), take the Flame about the Circle, then return to the Altar and kneel.

Take up the Cup with the Wine already in it, and your Athame. Place the Blade within the Cup, focus, and say:

The Cup is the Symbol of Woman and my Goddess!
The Athame is the Symbol of Man and my God!
Co-joined they are the Blessed Union
That produces the Three Drops of Inspiration,
The Creation Continuous!

Replace the Athame on the Altar, raise the Cup in honour of your Goddess and God, drink from it, take it to the West and go around the Circle, holding the Cup aloft, until the Circle is complete. Replace the Cup upon the Altar and take up your Staff once more.

Go to the Gate of Earth (symbolic place of Winter) and see the Gate. Raise the Staff aloft, and say:

Thee, I invoke, Great Uriel!
Open for me the Gate of Earth
As I link myself to the Whole
For this Time!
May the Elements of Earth attend with Me!
By Earth, By Sky, By Sea!
As I do Will, so mote it be!

Watch Him come in. Draw the sign of the Invoking Pentagram of Earth on the ether in front of you. He will mirror it from the Gate. Light the Elemental Candle.

Go to the Gate of Air (symbolic of the place of Spring) and see
the Gate. Raise the Staff aloft, and say:

**Thee, I invoke, Great Raphael!
Open for me the Gate of Air
As I link myself to the Whole
For this Time!
May the Elements of Air attend with Me!
By Earth, By Sky, By Sea!
As I do Will, so mote it be!**

Watch Him come in. Draw the sign of the Invoking Pentagram
of Air on the ether before you. He will mirror it from the Gate.
Light the Elemental Candle.

Go to the Gate of Fire (symbolic of the place of Summer) and see
the Gate. Raise the Staff aloft, and say:

**Come ye, Great Michael!
Open for me the Gate of Fire
As I link myself to the Whole
For this Time!
May the Elements of Fire attend with Me!
By Earth, By Sky, By Sea!
As I do Will, so mote it be!**

Watch Him come in. Draw the sign of the Invoking Pentagram
of Fire on the ether before you. He will mirror it from the Gate.
Light the Elemental Candle.

Go to the Gate of Water (symbolic of the place of Autumn) and
see the Gate. Raise the Staff aloft, and say:

**Thee I Invoke, Great Gabriel!
Open for me the Gate of Water
As I link myself to the Whole
For this Time!
May the Elements of Water attend with Me!
By Earth, By Sky, By Sea!
As I do Will, so mote it be!**

Watch Him come in. Draw the sign of the Invoking Pentagram of Water on the ether before you. He will mirror it from the Gate. Light the Elemental Candle and return to the Altar.

Sit down before the Altar. Be still. Listen to the Legend that you have recorded, 'Winter's End', *personalising with all the characters in the story*, for the entirety.

When you have done so and can feel the Force of your God within yourself, you will flow with whatever is correct until the natural conclusion.

✳ ✳ ✳

The Legend of Winter's End

'The castle stood high above a tor of living rock, seeming almost to grow from the rock itself. Around the ramparts the ceaseless, bitter wind smote and tore at the crumbling stone, whilst from below the Forest crept ever-closer, grasping and tugging with relentless green fingers at the ancient walls.

Even for the few, wrapped in furs and velvets, who stayed close to the roaring fires in tapestry-hung halls, the castle was a harsh and forbidding place. For the many who served the few it was a grim and merciless place indeed. The icy stillness within and the howling winds without seemed to penetrate the very soul and seek to extinguish the spark of life, and hope, therein.

The very nature of the place was inhospitable to man and wished him gone.

Within a room within the castle, one wall of which was hewn from the mountainside itself, a woman lay amongst a pile of soft, deep furs before a blazing fire. She was neither young nor old, seeming somewhere in Her middle years. Her face, though unlined, seemed ancient in its wisdom and Her deep, dark eyes held secrets that only great age can know. Her long dark hair was threaded here and there with silver. Her gaze fell steadily on the fire, seeming to seek an answer therein to the questions that Her troubled eyes asked.

There was a small sound behind Her in the room, and

although She did not turn around. Her eyes shifted focus and a small smile played about Her lips. "The door was locked," She announced quietly.

"Ah," a male voice answered, "I didn't think to try it. Did you seek to keep me out?"

"Would it have made any difference if I had?" She asked. There was a small silence.

"No," He replied pleasantly. The man did not move and His gaze upon the woman did not falter as the minutes passed. Still She did not turn around.

"How did you get in?" She asked at last. At that the man threw back His head and laughed loudly, exultantly.

"You didn't feel me coming!" He laughed, "You didn't know I was here!" He raised His fist and whooped boyishly. "Old woman," He said, "you're slipping!"

"You're heartless, Tohrn," the woman's voice was soft.

"I have no heart." He smiled as He said it.

"Ah, but that's not true," She replied, turning to face Him at last, "you have mine."

Their eyes met and held, Hers dark and shrouded, His clear, grey and open. Slowly Her gaze shifted as She took in every detail of His appearance. His hair and beard were thick and grey, the hair long and tousled, the beard, in contrast, short and neatly trimmed. His clothes were mainly leather, softened by years of wear and weather, rubbed smooth and shiny in some places, scuffed and roughened in others. His crumpled fur cloak was bedraggled, even torn in places, and His fur-lined boots were held together with crude leather thonging tied carelessly around the worst splits. The overall effect was distinctly shabby and unkempt.

"You look dreadful," She said, "and you've aged."

"Five years will do that to a man," He sighed ruefully, "and five years in your service will do it twice as quickly."

He moved then, striding across the room towards the fire. When He reached the fur rugs He bent to untie His boots and shrugged off His cloak, leaving them in an untidy heap on the floor as He folded His legs under Him to sit cross-legged on the floor, on the outer edge of the cosy half-circle of furs before the fire.

"Warm in here," He commented conversationally. "Babies are dying out there in the cold while you warm your arse in front of this fire." His eyes had taken on a flinty glint. There was a long, long silence in the room while the wind outside howled and moaned, biting with icy teeth at the thick tapestries hung before the window slits.

Without warning the woman sprang to Her feet, Her fists bunched tightly against Her thighs, and Her eyes bright with tears. "And do you think I never tire?" She cried, "Have you any idea how long I've been at this? You count your life from year to year, Tohrn, for years! I count mine in aeons that defy counting! My past stretches back into the dark mists before time began, and my future stretches forward . . ." Her voice broke into a sob, ". . . into eternity!" She buried Her face in Her hands, Her dark hair falling like a veil to hide Her anguish. "And I'm cold Tohrn; so cold I've forgotten how to warm the world!'

Had She been looking at Tohrn She would have seen the compassion and pain in His eyes and would have noticed the way His mouth moved several times before He could speak. She would have seen also the way He raised His hand as if to touch Her before letting it fall back to His knees again. None of this did She see, but heard She only His words:

"Don't talk to me about eternities! Seven years of Winter is a bloody eternity to a peasant girl watching baby after baby die in the snow that fills her croft!" He managed to speak all this quietly.

"Tohrn, don't!" She whispered.

"The Forest itself is crying out its suffering," He continued, "as it sees the animals die for want of food and shelter. The trees, of course, may never recover."

"Tohrn, stop!" She cried, "I command your silence!"

"Oh, I don't obey your commands anymore. Didn't I tell you?" He said softly before continuing relentlessly. "Did you know the people still revere your Sacred Forest and have cut no trees to burn to stay alive?" He asked. "Amazing, that! Oh, and you'll be pleased to know that the wolves still live," He went on, His words dropping like blows upon Her bowed head. "You see, the ground is now too hard to bury the dead; frozen solid, you see, so the people just leave them at the edge of the Forest for the wolves to eat."

At this moment the woman dropped to the floor and held Her hands out as if to ward him off. "Spare me this, Tohrn," She sobbed, "if you love me still just a little, spare me this!"

"Love you?" His calm broke and He rose with one quick, fluid movement. "What does it matter if *I* love you?" He strode to the window slit and ripped aside the covering tapestry. He gestured outside. "They love you still, though why I cannot imagine! Do you no longer hear their callings and supplications? Do you not see the offerings laid upon every household shrine? Can you not feel the grief and bewilderment in every heart? Damn it, woman," He leapt across the rugs and grasped Her wrist in a cruel grip and, wrenching Her towards Himself, He spat the words with icy rage into Her upturned face, "they love you still and blame themselves!"

The woman's countenance changed then, Her face becoming calm and still; Her eyes slipped out of focus and seemed to gaze inwards with deadly intent. Her form began to shimmer and waver, changing before His eyes. Her skin hung dry and wrinkled, Her hair fell in grey wisps from Her bowed head. The ancient Crone raised a gnarled finger before the man's face and spoke in a whisper, like the wind amongst dry leaves. "Young man, thou treadest too far! Thou darest to question *my* right to destroy that which I have created, and withdraw my hand from upon the Earth. *Mine* is the power of life and death, and though it grieves me an end will come to all things. If I decree that endless Winter shall blight this land, then so shall it be until I decree it otherwise!"

To her utter amazement the man smiled, then laughed! Still holding Her wrist He raised His other hand and held it high above His head. "Oh no, old woman," He laughed, "you're old and tired and know not how to change. The world needs no more of you! Spring will come with the coming of the Virgin, soft and supple and eager. We can bring warmth and life to the frozen world outside, if I can but thaw your icy heart . . . and methinks I could rise to the occasion!" He laughed again.

"*You* Tohrn?" the Crone shrieked scornfully, "Oh, I think not!" But Her derisive cackle was cut short as the man before Her raised His face and began the Invocations. The woman gasped in astonishment as She watched the changes taking place in the man's appearance.

The Power seemed to dance and hum around Him, like a blue flame flickering eagerly over His form. The light then changed to a glorious green and the air smelled of the fresh, earthy smells of Spring. The Promise. Surely those were horns sprouting from the man's head! And behind Him a golden light and a soft warmth, pulsing and shining and bathing Him in its mellow glow.

The Words flowed on from His lips, His strong, rich voice filling the room. The wind outside ceased howling and the whole world seemed to be holding its breath.

The old Crone no longer resisted but stood mesmerised, gazing intently, almost reverently, into the man's exultant face. Suddenly His eyes flew open and He looked directly at Her. He began the final Invocation, Power throbbing with His every heartbeat, and the Crone's form began to change once more.

When Tohrn stopped speaking His head slumped briefly whilst He calmed His short, rasping breaths. His hand was still closed about His Lady's wrist and it was to this hand that His gaze first shifted.

Her fingers fluttered painfully, soft, smooth, white fingers with rosy pink nails. He released Her and She laid Her hand in His. He raised His eyes to Her face then, His lips curving into a boyish smile as He beheld the fresh young Maiden before Him. A faint blush touched Her creamy cheeks and Her trembling lips tried hard to smile. Twining His rough fingers into Her thick, soft hair He bent His head to whisper something close to Her ear. His other hand moved down Her throat, pushing Her robe away from Her shoulder, to find Her young breast. He smothered Her gasp with a kiss and laid Her gently down among the furs. He surprised Himself. After the Invocations He had thought His strength was spent, yet it would seem it was not so. His passion was just not His own, for the whole world had waited long for this moment, and He abandoned Himself to it with joy and reverence.

He recollected Himself briefly as the girl beneath Him cried out, "Tohrn, please . . . remember I am a Virgin!" but by and large it was a Ritual performed with a creditable and holy zeal!

When it was over and the Man and the Woman lay drowsily in each others' arms, the dull, grey clouds parted briefly as a thin Wintry Sun shone weakly across the land. They did not see it, of course; for the moment They saw only each other . . . but who would gainsay Them that moment? The Man would all too soon grow old and die, the Woman lose Him as She had lost so many. Life goes on, the seasons change, whole worlds come and go, but She will ever remain.

And if, from time to time, She grows too tired to warm the World, let there always be Men of faith and courage to warm and renew Her heart with Love.'

* * *

You will then take up the Cup of consecrated Wine, sprinkle a little on the Ritual Cakes and drink from the Cup. If there is another or others with you, you will share the Cakes and Wine with them.

Check that the Brazier or Fireplace is ready, and light the wood from the Altar Candle, saying:

I light the Beacon that Lights the World!
The Seasons change, the Roots of Life!
In honour of my Ancient Inheritance!
True freedom to Dance Within the Earth,
And Upon the Earth,
And Above the Earth,
With All who Dance to the Piper!

Take the consecrated Oil and rub some on your feet, saying:

Blessed be these feet made to walk the Path of the High Gods!

Rub some on your knees, saying:

Blessed be these knees made to kneel at the Altar of Infinity!

Rub some on your genitals, saying:

Blessed be this phallus which gives life to the Unborn!

Rub some on your chest, saying;

Blessed be this breast within which beats my Strength!

Rub some just above your lips, saying;

Blessed be these lips made only to speak the Truth of the Lady and Lord of All Living!

Note If there is a Priestess with you you will share the Fivefold Kiss (lips, not oil) with her, exchanging 'phallus' for 'womb', and 'strength' for 'beauty' — she is to share the kiss with you as above.

To complete the Rite you will raise the Staff aloft and say:

Complete this ending on the never-ending spiral!
The Sacred Seed beneath the Snow!
The Time of the Sun King is the Time
Of the Some Become One!
I call Blessed the Darkness as I call Blessed the Light!

The Rite of Winter is done.

Go to the Gateway in order of the beginning and pay honour to the Archangelic Lords and the Elementals attending, dismiss Them with the Banishing Pentagram as you have been taught, and extinguish the Candle there. Reverse the Circle. Allow the Altar Candle to burn down. Record your personal observations and experiences.

Follow the Ritual with as much celebrating as you can, with much music.

Ritual of Spring Equinox

(appropriate time to work: Dawn)

Set up your Temple in the usual manner and bathe with intent of purification.

When you are ready you will seat yourself before the Altar, light the Altar Candle and the Incense, and centre yourself by using four-fold breathing leading to a soft humming-chant.

Use your Staff to cast the Circle about yourself, saying:

O Place of Power,
Outside of Time!
Keep all within and all without
And forge a Barrier between the Two!
I seek the Place beyond the Veil:
O Spear of Light I summon thee
In the Names of the Lady and Lord of All Life!
By Earth, By Sky, By Sea!
So mote it be!

Return to the Altar and take up the Salt in its container and deposit it into the Pentacle. Place the tip of your Athame Blade within it, and say:

Blessings be upon thee,
Symbol of Earth,
Forced from the Womb of the Mother
By the Might of the Sacred Sun!

Draw down the blue light from your Blade and infuse the Salt with it. When it is done replace the Pentacle on the Altar and take up the container of Water. Place the tip of your Athame Blade within it, call down the blue light, and say:

Out of thee Water Creature,

Goes all that is not pure!
May only the Essence of the Great Mother remain!

Now add the Salt to the Water and stir them.

   Begin, at the place of the South (North in the northern lands) and sprinkle the boundary of your Circle with the consecrated Water. When the revolution is complete return the Water to the Altar and take up the Incense. Begin at the East and Cense the Circle. Return the Censer to the Altar and take up the Altar Candle. Begin at the North (South in the northern lands) and take the Candle about the Circle.

   Return to the Altar and kneel. Take up the Cup (with the Wine in it) and your Athame. Place the Blade within its depths, focus, and say:

The Cup is the Symbol of Woman and my Goddess!
The Athame is as Man and my God!
Co-joined they are the Blessed Union
That produces the Three Drops of Inspiration,
The Creation Continuous!

Replace the Athame upon the Altar, raise the Cup in honour of your Goddess and God, drink from it, then take it to the West and go about the Circle, holding it aloft, until the Circle is complete. Replace the Cup upon the Altar and take up your Staff once more.

   Go to the Gate of Air (symbolic of the place of Spring) and see the Gate before you. Raise the Staff aloft, and say:

Thee, I invoke, Great Raphael!
Open for me the Gate of Air
As I link myself to the Whole
For this Time!
May the Elements of Air attend with Me!
By Earth, By Sky, By Sea!
As I do Will, so mote it be!

Watch Him come in. Draw the sign of the Invoking Pentagram of Air on the ether before you. He will mirror it from the Gate.

Light the Candle.

Go to the Gate of Fire (symbolic of the Summer) and see the Gate before you. Raise the Staff aloft, and say:

Thee, I invoke, Great Michael!
Open for me the Gate of Fire
As I link myself to the Whole
For this Time!
May the Elements of Fire attend with Me!
By Earth, By Sky, By Sea!
As I do Will, so mote it be!

Watch Him come in. Draw the sign of the Invoking Pentagram of Fire on the ether before you. He will mirror it from the Gate.
    Light the Candle.

Go to the Gate of Water (symbolic of Autumn) and see the Gate before you. Raise the Staff aloft, and say:

Thee, I invoke, Great Gabriel!
Open for me the Gate of Water
As I link myself to the Whole
For this Time!
May the Elements of Water attend with Me!
By Earth, By Sky, By Sea!
As I do Will, so mote it be!

Watch Him come in. Draw the sign of the Invoking Pentagram of Water on the ether in front of you. He will mirror it from the Gate.
    Light the Candle.

Go to the Gate of Earth (symbolic of Winter) and see the Gate before you. Raise the Staff aloft, and say:

Thee, I invoke, Great Uriel!
Open for me the Gate of Earth

As I link myself to the Whole
For this Time!
May the Elements of Earth attend Me!
By Earth, By Sky, By Sea!
As I do Will, so mote it be!

Watch Him come in. Draw the sign of the Invoking Pentagram of Earth on the ether before you, and He will mirror it from the Gate.

Light the Candle.

Return to the Altar. Now sit down and be still. Listen to the Legend that you have recorded, 'Spring Equinox', *personalising with all the characters in the story*. When it is complete and you can feel the Force of your God within you, you will flow with whatever is appropriate until the natural conclusion.

※　※　※

The Legend of Spring Equinox

'Eleanora, the blacksmith's daughter, was quite lovely, yet why, it is hard to say exactly — her hair was long and reddish-gold of colour but coarse and wild, beyond hope of braids or coils; her eyes were tawny and glowed with green lights when she ran in the Forest or lay down within the lush, green grass — the lashes were, unfortunately, the same colour as her hair, and her small, angular face was splashed with freckles. Her tiny frame was but sparsely covered with flesh and she had none of the enticing curves and roundnesses that the other village girls so liked to flaunt.

The blacksmith was a large, hearty man, hugely muscled as blacksmiths inevitably are. His wife matched his form, not in muscle but in soft, rounded flesh; from her round, laughing face with its quivering chins to her broad backside, more like the rump of a carthorse than any plausible part of female anatomy. Eleanora had four brothers, all older than she was, all attaining a stature to rival their father's and a disposition as placid and invariably cheerful as their mother's.

Their little sister, by contrast, was quick-tongued and quick-

137

tempered, always darting about and scolding like a small, bright-eyed bird. Her family had long since abandoned all hope of 'breaking' this filly to harness, and by and large she was left to follow her inspirations and enthusiasms as a butterfly follows the lure of a field of spring flowers.

The deep woods near Eleanora's village were her special domain. Indeed, she ventured deeper into the Forest than any other female had dared to go, and only the hunters, in safe numbers, had ever trod upon the Forest floor in places that Eleanora knew well. The extent of her ramblings she naturally kept secret from her family, yet she knew that she was utterly safe within the dark, green depths — *how* she knew this she could not say, nor in fact had she ever paused to consider.

The villagers were full of excitement and a spirit of festivity on this particular day. The Equinox of Spring was upon them and the air was full of the sweet smells and sounds of newly-awakened life. The sun was warm and bright, the earth covered with young, green growth everywhere, and tender spring flowers and blossoms added splashes of colour.

With a perversity typical of her, Eleanora found the gaiety and activity of her fellows irritating, and rather than trying to match her mood to theirs she became restless and withdrawn, feeling a strange yearning.

Fleeing from the joyous preparations in the village for the Rite of Spring which was to take place that evening, she took refuge in the deep, cool stillness of her beloved Forest.

Delving much deeper and further than she had ever gone before she seemed drawn by some relentless, irresistible force that left her trembling with both fear and anticipation. Eventually she ran herself to a standstill, coming to rest by a small, brackish pool in a sun-dappled clearing. She knew that she was lost, but as she threw herself down on the soft, cool moss beneath the trees she pushed the unpleasant thought from her, resolving to think about it later.

At first she heard nothing but the thudding of her own heart and the rasp of her own gasping breath, but as these calmed she began to listen to the sounds of the Forest — the whispers of soft breezes amongst the leaves, the gentle plop and ripple of the water-life of the pool, the ecstatic bursts of song from this bird and that, outdoing each other in contests of beauty and joy — but more than this, the Forest itself seemed to hum with a voice of its own, a deeply resonant, compelling drone that thrummed at the very earth beneath her.

Eleanora had been dozing contentedly when she became awake to a prickling sensation of unease that crept across her body. Lying perfectly still, completely awake now, she held her breath and listened. She could sense that she was no longer alone in the clearing, yet could see nothing. A flicker of movement here and there teased at her peripheral vision, yet eluded her direct gaze.

She was surrounded, but by what, or whom, she could not tell! Then, to her utter astonishment, she heard the sound of pipes being played quite close by in the Forest. Her first thought was one of relief as she hoped that rescue was at hand, but then she realised that she had *never* heard any human play the pipes like this! The haunting, impossibly beautiful melody drifted around her like a mist, seeming to lay an enchantment upon her mind. Eleanora found it impossible to remain alert, on guard for the unseeing beings in the trees all around her, as the music seduced her mind into awareness of only itself.

Gradually, one by one, little folk began to emerge into the clearing. Closer they drew and closer, until Eleanora could clearly see their soft, brown, hazel or green eyes and long pointed ears, their tiny hands and dainty, leather-shod feet. As she lay, propped up on an elbow, the Elfin-folk stood around her in a Circle, close enough to touch. Some hid, one behind the other, some held hands while others, a little braver, reached out to stroke her skin before quickly withdrawing again. Still spell-bound by wonder of this, Eleanora glanced beyond the Circle of faces around her to see deer and squirrel, foxes and a myriad of small creatures and birds cluster around the edge of the clearing.

On and on the pipes played, a ceaseless melody that tugged

the heart and caressed the soul. Many of the Elven-ones now came forward to touch and stroke her, their touch soft and gentle but surprisingly sensual. Eleanora smiled shakily at them and was rewarded with shy grins, illuminating every face in return; and all the while the sound of piping grew closer and closer. The little folk stirred and murmured, their excitement and anticipation obvious. They did not cease their caresses, however, and while one part of Eleanora's mind was screaming a warning, her body yearned for more. Suddenly the piping ceased and with a cry of joy from the Elves a figure strode into the clearing, before Eleanora's incredulous stare.

The figure was tall, with dark, curling hair running riotously into an equally dark and curly beard. His skin seemed toned with the colours of earth, and His eyes were a deep, velvety brown. His smile was wide and matched the humorous, wicked glint in His eye. The magnificent spread of horns rising from beneath His hair seemed not at all incongruous, rather entirely appropriate; His body was lean and hard, covered in fine, dark hair, and the hands that still held the pipes were smooth and well formed. His powerful thighs rippled with strength and His legs, surprisingly hairy, ended not with a human foot but, inevitably, with a cloven hoof. He was quite naked and His magnificent phallus hung heavily below a riot of dark, soft curls. He strode over to where Eleanora lay, while the Elves laughed and chattered at Him in a strange, birdlike tongue. The looks on their faces as they gazed up at Him were rapturous and adoring.

As He reached the girl's feet He dropped to one knee and gently laid a hand upon her thigh. The look with which He returned her startled gaze was a mixture of humour, wonderment and sheer carnal lust! By now the touch of the little folk had elicited a response from Eleanora's body which she scarcely believed possible, and the look she gave the figure before her, as she reached out her hand to Him, was a frank invitation. At this, the Elves flew into a frenzy of delight, hugging and kissing each other with abandon.

Cernunnos leant across Eleanora, His eyes not leaving her

140

face until His lips found hers. Her arms rose tentatively to encircle those broad shoulders, her fingers then hooked themselves into His long, dark hair to pull His head more firmly down towards her.

She was dimly aware that the Elves were divesting her of all her clothing, but the faraway feeling of vulnerability was soon replaced by a much nearer, more urgent emotion. She could feel his entire body now, which lay covering hers on the soft, green moss. His hands, though moving slowly and gently, seemed everywhere at once; a light, feathery touch here, a deep firm caress there. His mouth, likewise, kissed and sucked ceaselessly, seeming to want to taste every part of her. As her heart beat wildly she became aware of His hard, erect phallus pressed against her body. Her excitement was tempered with fear as, tiny as she was, she contemplated the impossibility of what was about to happen. His touch was becoming insistent as, moaning softly, He gathered her up against Him in a powerful grasp. He smelled of earth and fresh, green leaves and the sweet, musky smell of the Forest animals, and it seemed to Eleanora that He became her entire universe. Her whole past and all her possible futures were crystallised into the moment. Almost without conscious thought she felt her legs part willingly under His tense, probing body, felt the intense excitement as His gentle fingers drew apart the lips of her vulva and He momentarily laid His throbbing penis against her. He was so gentle, so infinitely tender — His body piercing hers was an ecstasy made all the sweeter for the stab of pain, and the flood of sensation that followed carried her upwards on a tide of joy that eventually broke like the crashing of waves on a bright and distant shore.

It had to end, of course. With murmuring caresses and sleepy kisses, her body languidly entwined in His, the late afternoon sun slanted down through the trees to bathe them both in mellow, golden light. Eventually He rose; Eleanora gasped and reached for Him, unable to let Him go. The thought of their separation brought sudden tears stinging to her eyes and her heart felt that it would shatter into a thousand pieces.

Cernunnos raised her face to look at Him, her small, pointed chin lost in His hand. He gazed long into her eyes, a quizzical eyebrow raised, with a crooked, seemingly self-mocking smile, His expression holding true regret. He raised His pipes to His lips and began to play a strange melody and He watched as Eleanora's eyes drooped and closed.

When she slept the Elves rushed forward to wash and dress her, and straighten her hair. They led her, unresisting, from the glade, and the Horned Figure watched them go and sighed deeply before turning and striding back into the Forest.

At the edge of the Forest the Elves left her to awaken, shortly, from her trance.

Eleanora felt confused, not remembering how she came to be there, but with her mind full of images as tantalizingly elusive as a half-remembered melody she rubbed her face into full wakefulness.

With merry cries a group of young people from the village saw her where she now stood. They ran to meet her, laughing and chattering, and strung garlands of fresh flowers around her hair and neck.

"Come, Eleanora!" they cried, " 'Tis the Sacred Spring Day! We need you before the Rite can begin!" '

* * *

You will then take up the Cup of consecrated Wine, sprinkle a little onto the Cakes and drink from the Cup. If there is another or others with you, share the Cakes and Wine with them.

Check that the Brazier or Fireplace is ready and light the wood from the Altar Candle, saying:

I light the Beacon that Lights the World!
The Seasons change, the Flower of Life!
In honour of my Ancient Inheritance!
True Freedom to Dance within the Earth,
And upon the Earth,
And above the Earth,
With All who Dance to the Piper!

Take the consecrated oil and rub some on your feet, saying:

Blessed be these feet made to walk the Path of the High Gods!

Rub some on your knees, saying;

Blessed be these knees made to kneel at the Altar of Infinity!

Rub some on your genitals, saying:

Blessed be this phallus which gives life to the Unborn!

Rub some on your chest, saying:

Blessed be this breast within which beats my Strength!

Rub some just above your lips, saying:

Blessed be these lips made only to speak the Truth of the Lady and Lord of All Living!

Note If you are with a Priestess you will share the Fivefold Kiss with her, exchanging 'phallus; for 'womb', and 'strength' for 'beauty'. She will then return the Kiss as above.

To complete the Rite you will raise your Staff aloft, and say:

The coming together with the Sun Child at the Time of Manhood
With the Priestess of the Moon
Is His Initiation into the Realm of the High King!
All upon the Earth is at One with this Divine Union,
The Fruit of Magic.
The Union of Male and Female is the Glorification
Of the Island-Outside-Of-Time!
The Great Stag hunts the Great Stag
And the Daughters of the Goddess call the Tune!

The Rite of Spring is done. Go to each Gateway in the order of the beginning and pay honour to the Archangelic Forces and the Elementals attending, dismiss them with the Banishing Pentagram of the pertinent Element, and extinguish the Candles.

Reverse the Circle. Allow the Altar Candle to burn down.

Record your impressions and experiences in your Grimoir, and plan to have a party in the evening!

Ritual of Summer Solstice
Ritual of Autumn Equinox

The Rituals of Summer and Autumn can follow the format laid down for Winter and Spring, with the following changes associated with the season:

Summer Solstice
For Summer you will begin the Summoning of the Archangelic Lords by invoking Michael first.

When you light the Brazier or Fireplace/pit you will say:

I light the Beacon that Lights the World!
The Seasons change, the Fruit of Life!
In honour of my Ancient Inheritance!
True Freedom to Dance with the Earth,
And on the Earth,
And above the Earth,
With All who Dance to the Piper!

And your concluding Invocation will be:

Great One!
Great King of the Sun!
Lord of the Flame!
Powers of Light summoned through Life!
I summon thee to within thy Lands!
Artu! Llugh! Cernunnos! Balin! Herne!
The Power of Peace, the Flower of Truth!
Great Temple of Stars I bid thee come!

The Legend of Summer, named 'The Chosen One', that you are to tape for the Summer Solstice is as follows:

* * *

The Legend of the Chosen One
Part 1 (Summer)

'The man whom other men had called Hu: he who had been the Chosen One, stood alone upon a rocky rise, surveying the Forest before him. Behind him the icy waters of the Northern Sea could be clearly seen, and smelled clean and tangy of the fresh breeze. The Forest of great Pines stretched forth before him, and to his left and to his right the Forest spread, and there where the land met the sky on the distant horizon was there naught but the Forest.

The wind whipped cruelly through his newly cropped hair and beard, and once again, involuntarily, his hand reached up to touch the remaining hair on scalp and face. Until yesterday neither his hair nor his beard had ever been cut — long, blonde braids had hung to below his waist, and his coarse yellow beard was customarily tucked into his broad leather belt, there to keep company with the fearsome array of weaponry that also dwelt therein.

He was young, having seen but eighteen summers, and was as tall and as strong as a young fir tree. His eyes, the colour of the foam-flecked, booming sea, gazed unseeing across the treetops as his thoughts pondered upon the events of the day and night just passed.

Yesterday he had been the Chosen One, the Sun King, feted and honoured among his people, the golden boy upon whom all the hope of the coming year was fixed. Today he stood, solitary, on a lonely, windswept tor; no hair, no name, no future that he could see.

He felt like a small, lost child and to his shame he felt the sharp sting of tears behind his eyes. His mind, as if set on a course he was powerless to alter, began again to relive the confused memories of the last twenty-four hours. He remembered quite clearly the games of skill and mock battles taking place in the bright, early sunshine of the midsummer day. He had excelled, as always, seeming invincible as he laughed his way from victory to victory, a living triumph of youth and strength.

"Child of the Gods!" the people had murmured. Then noon-time had come and the atmosphere of the celebrations had changed subtly, as the Sun achieved His zenith. The air had been charged with expectation, the energies of the midsummer festivities intensified and seemed to hang suspended like a palpable force in the still, noon warmth.

The Priestesses had come for him then, garlanding him and paying him great honour before leading him away . . . to an eerie, dark place in the Forest, where sacred trees grew close in a grove, and an ancient altar stood rooted into the soft, green turf. He had been given warm wine to drink, into which he had seen the High Priestess crumble some dry and pungent fungi. Upon drinking the wine he had felt his senses heighten and sharpen, and he became acutely aware of every sound, sight, smell and touch. His mind, in contrast, felt distant and confused, coherent thought eluded him and concentration seemed impossible. He recalled the High Priestess standing before him, shimmering with power and presence, holding out her arms in invocation, as the other women danced in sacred steps around her. When she spoke her voice rang clear and bell-like, echoing in the dark woods and rising in a spiral of power to the bright sky above:

"I am, Anu, Goddess of Air, Ruler of Earth and Sky and the Dark Realm Beyond! Creator of Life! Bringer of Death! It is I to whom the Gods of men shall answer! It is I for whom the Gods of men shall live and die! And thus, according to my command, has the mighty Sun God, God of the Sky, risen in His glory, shining forth upon the Earth, bringing warmth and light, and sending down the rain to bring forth Life unto His Beloved."

She had come forward to kneel at the man's feet.

"O Mighty One that men call Beli, but Who is known to us by many Sacred Names, God of the Sun and Sky, of Lightning and Thunder and Rain, Bringer of rich harvests and Provider of plenteous game, we bring before thee Bride, Thy beloved Earth; bless Her Lord, that we be blessed, and that Thou, too, be ever-blessed upon the lips of men!"

He remembered succumbing to the drug he had been given

147

and swaying on his feet, squinting his eyes against the painfully intense sunlight, sweating profusely in the incredible heat that surrounded and suffused his body. A young Priestess had been brought before him, her hands and lips cool upon his face and body. The other Priestesses, lost in a communion of heart and spirit, chanted and stamped in a slow, steady rhythm that seemed like the heartbeat of the Earth herself.

Here the young man paused in his thoughts, shivering slightly although the day was not cold. He had lain with the girl there, on the soft moss beneath the trees, murmuring her name as she whispered his — the Sacred Names of the Gods within each other were what they whispered — God of Sun and Sky, Goddess of Earth, who co-joined to bring forth life and blessedness. There had been more drugged wine, confusing further his already numbed mind.

As the Sun had sunk below the treetops the Ritual had continued. The holy women had formed the shape of a boat around him, their undulating bodies mimicking perfectly the motion of the Sea. The High Priestess, standing where the prow of the boat would be, held her arms high in invocation once more. She spoke of the Sun's waning strength and of His voyage into the Underworld of Annwn and of darkness. She spoke of the Quest He must undertake to renew His spirit so that He could return, once again, to rule the Sky.

All this the man recalled, and how he had then felt tired, confused, and had longed for release — and release was soon upon him.

Striding forward, the High Priestess had held high a long, two-edged Knife. "Thou hast no Name! Thou art the Chosen One!" she cried as she had cut through his beard. "Thou hast no People! Thou art the Sacrificed One!" she cried as she had hacked off his hair. "Thou art most blessed and honoured of men!" she said as she held the Knife to his breast.

Blackness, numbness, quiet, peace.

He had awoken as the Sun's first rays tipped the treetops. The women had slept, exhausted, wrapped in their cloaks around the Altar. His body was stiff and cold and he felt ill from the after-effects of the drugged wine. He rose shakily to his feet. The High Priestess was aware of him first and stood staring at him, a frown between her brows. The other women, one by one, woke up to gaze at him with unreadable expressions in their guarded eyes. He broke the eerie silence, addressing the High Priestess.

"Holy Mother," his voice sounded thin and weak, "I am cold and weary and would seek a warm fire and a fur robe. Is it fitting now that I return?"

"Return?" she had replied, "I do not understand — to where would you return?"

"Home, Mother! Can I go home now?" He felt a touch of fear on his spine.

The woman spoke softly "Oh, you do not understand at all, do you small one? You are the Chosen One, the Sacrificed One. There can be no returning for you. Your Quest is upon you. Your journey lies in quite another direction now."

He shook his head, trying to clear the last of the cobwebs from his mind. The other women had drifted away, wraith-like, into the trees, and only the High Priestess had remained with him. She beckoned him to follow her and led him through secret Forest pathways until they came to the tor upon which he now stood.

"'Tis the Hill of Vision!" she had told him.

Pointing westward over the vast, dark, primordial Forests she spoke a last time: "Follow the setting Sun. There will be Those who will come for you. I cannot help you further."

And then he was alone.

And thus he stood for a long, long time, feeling his very soul shift on its axis to spin a new Pattern and weave a new thread.

Into the Forest of Souls' Winter he stepped, knowing not what lay before him, nor yet who he was, nor what he was to become.

But there were those in the Forest who knew, and watched, and waited . . .'

* * *

Autumn Equinox

For Autumn you will begin the summoning of the Archangelic Lords by invoking Gabriel (of the West) first.

When you light the Brazier or the Fireplace/pit you will say:

I light the Beacon that Lights the World!
The Seasons change, the Seeds of Life!
In honour of my Ancient Inheritance!
True Freedom to Dance within the Earth,
And upon the Earth,
And above the Earth,
With All who Dance to the Piper!

And your concluding Invocation will be:

The God of Light dwells Enthroned
Within the Labyrinth of Future and Past.
He dwells with the Dragon and the Lady of the Deep!
Secret Seed! Seed of Earth, Seed of Flesh, Seed of Stars,
The Crystal Seed of Fire!
Sacred is Life, even in Death,
For One is One and One is the Other,
And together they are the Three Drops of Inspiration,
Creation Continuous.

*   *   *

The Legend of the Forest of Souls' Winter
Part 2 (Autumn)

'How shall I speak to thee of the man who trod once upon the secret, sacred Forest paths? He who had no Name; for his name that once was had been taken from him, and his Name that was to be had not yet been spoken. Let me just call him "the man", for that is how we knew him then, and when we spoke of him amongst ourselves, we of the Forest, that is what we called him.

I am Ulrika, which means "Wolf-power", for Wolf I be. Sometimes. Sometimes I am otherwise . . . but I will tell thee of it so that the man will be remembered and his deeds known to those who are of his Kind.

I first saw him as he stood upon the rocky rise at the edge of the Forest, my home. I had never seen a man so closely before and in truth I thought him beautiful. There was a strangeness about him that I did not understand, as if he carried his soul on the outside, instead of the inside, naked for all to see.

We sent the Raven to him where he stood, for the Raven is sacred to the Gods he served, and he followed her into the Forest . . . we had hoped he would, we who waited in the shadow of the trees. His stumbling footsteps did not carry him far that day, his weariness overcoming him, and he soon lay down to sleep upon the soft, dry litter beneath the trees. The Wudu-Maer, our Forest Mother, spoke softly into our hearts and bid us guard him through the night, as long as he slept.

He wept in his sleep in the darkness, and the Wudu-Maer gathered his tears in a silver chalice that shone white among the stars in the dark night sky.

When he woke he followed his Raven-sister as she flew low from branch to branch and led him to the stream of the Waters of Life. He smiled at her as she perched close to him.

"Little sister," he said, "in the Name of the Gods do I thank thee," and thereby won her heart. The Waters of Life renewed his strength and he turned inwards into the Forest.

And so his journey began, and the first of his Companions flew by his side. It was the season of plenty, when the Sun rides high in the sky, and the Forest yielded up to him nuts and berries to fill his belly, and fine branches aplenty for the making of bow and shaft. Occasionally he took himself a small animal to eat of its flesh and use its skin to clothe his body . . . such is the way of all life, and the Wudu-Maer begrudged him not.

All this time I, Ulrika, had followed him, keeping careful watch over him, warning away my curious brethren with my long, yellow teeth and my eloquent snarl . . . but at night as he slept the man shivered as the wolf-calls echoed around the Forest, and although he did not understand the language he could not mistake the meaning.

So my silent vigil ended, and I came forth into his presence that he might know me. I came to him as he prepared his single daily meal; our eyes met over his small fire, and I was afraid — not of harm but of rejection. He looked gravely into my eyes and asked, "What took you so long?" and laughed. It is hard to remain dignified when joy overtakes one. And so it was that the second of his Companions, I, Ulrika, walked at his side.

Summer is but a short season in our land, and shorter still within the dark depths of the Forest, and soon the days grew noticeably shorter and the nights fell long and cold. The man, the Raven and I spent our days journeying deeper into the Forest, which seemed to grow wilder and darker with every step we took. Even I, the Wolf who belongs here, began to feel the Presence pressing gently upon us, like the whisper of breath upon the nape of one's neck.

It was about this time that the first Challenge came upon the man. Towards the end of a wearisome afternoon, as the sun dipped low behind the trees and we began to seek a safe place to spend the night, a mighty roaring and breaking of branches was heard behind us. We had barely time to prepare ourselves for a fight when Brufus, our brother Bear, charged us from the trees.

He was up on his hind legs, his forepaws slashing at the air before him, his long, white teeth gnashing and snapping in his gaping, foaming mouth, and his angry eyes burned with amber fire. The Raven flew at his head while I rushed forward to defend the man with all the speed and skill of my Kind that I could muster. Brufus, however, cared nothing for me or the Raven, seeking only to destroy the human intruder he saw before him.

The man, grabbing his crudely fashioned bow, sprang nimbly to the branches of the nearest tree. He was hoisting himself to safety with brother Bear breathing hotly at his heels when the branch from which he was hanging snapped! In desperation I dove forward again, managing but a single rip at the towering, massive thigh of the Bear before he opened up my side with a single slash from his wicked claw. I lay in agony and despair, my life's blood gushing from me, expecting naught now but to see my beloved's gory death before my glazed eyes.

The man now lay in a crumpled heap at Brufus' feet, feeling around him desperately for his spilled arrows. Brother Bear roared above him, huge paws poised to strike, his huge head, with its dripping, open jaws, weaving from side to side. Suddenly a voice was heard above the sound of the Bear's deep, rumbling growls; a woman's voice!

"Brufus!" the voice was calm, clear and commanding. "Hearken to me, Brufus, my son!"

The Bear, his muzzle wrinkling as he sought her scent, dropped to all fours and turned to face her. I also turned my head where I lay, to gaze in wonderment . . . 'twas the Wudu-Maer, the Forest Mother Herself, who stood tall and terrible, Her long, moss-coloured hair flowing over Her fur robes. Her skin was the colour of Earth and Autumn leaves, and in Her gnarled hand She carried a mysterious Staff, deeply carven.

Brufus, his snarls and growls becoming grunts and whimpers of appeasement, shambled over to where She stood and grovelled at Her feet. She reached forward to caress the mighty head, but Her voice, when She spoke, was stern.

"The season grows cold, and you will soon seek your Cave, and sleep. Yet I find you here, raging through my Forest, thinking to strike at the very fabric of My Divine Weaving! The man is *mine*, Brufus, he is the Chosen One! His life is not yours, nor even his own, to take! To make restitution, therefore, for that which you sought to do, you shall walk as his Companion, so that you might learn what he is, and thereby know more fully what *you* are!"

I thought then that She would leave, and my heart ached that She should go, but instead She turned and came to where I lay.

"Little Wolf-daughter," She said softly, "you have given up your heart to this man as readily as you have given up your body. I can mend your body, Ulrika, but your heart will be broken more cruelly than your body can ever be, and I can mend it not for you." So saying, She laid Her hand on my torn side and instantly it was healed ... then She was gone.

The man, throughout all this, remained quiet and still, and later that night when sleep should have overtaken him he was thoughtful and distant. He dwelt deeply within himself, not troubling to make up the fire or to eat. Once I saw him hold out his hands before him and turn them this way and that as if he had never seen them before. I crept closer to nuzzle against his knee, but for once he did not acknowledge me.

On and deeper into the Forest of Souls' Winter the Quest continued, though we who were the Companions knew not for what we Quested, neither, I think, at this time did the man, whose Quest it was. We were drawing close to the very heart of the Forest, where the Wudu-Maer Herself dwelt, where time becomes elusive and the borders of reality shift and change. The nights were becoming truly cold, and one morning we awoke to find the Forest had been touched by the first frost. The man raised his face to the cold north wind.

"The Frost-giants come, and will soon walk upon these paths by our sides as we journey. When winter is come, what then, my friends? You must seek out a warm place to shield you from the passage of the Winter Queen. You cannot remain abroad when She walks the Forest, and I would not ask it of you."

"But what of you?" my eyes sought his and asked the question.

"I know not yet where I will be, but not here, I feel. Ulrika, have you noticed that I have not eaten for many, many days and yet I hunger not? And even when you and Brufus shiver 'neath your fur I feel nothing of the cold? My spirit seems to fly and soar around me as freely as does my sister Raven, and is bound no longer in this insubstantial body. And yet ... something keeps me here. What is it?" I could not answer him.

His answer came, though he did not at first recognise it, when we first perceived the Stag shadowing our path in the cover of the trees. I have seen many stags in my life, and am likely to see many more, but never have I seen this beast's equal, nor do I think I will again. He stood tall and was powerfully built, with massive shoulder and haunch. His head was broad and powerfully held on an immensely muscled neck. Above, a magnificent spread of majestic antlers proclaimed his might and power. He watched our small group with a gleaming, hostile eye, and every now and then he bellowed a challenge, seemingly directed at the man in our midst. He dogged our footsteps for many days, and although he never came close nor made any offer of friendship, it seemed as if he became, perhaps, the most significant of the Companions.

Thus it was that we came to the very heart of the Forest, where the stream we call the Waters of Life springs from the heart of the Earth Herself and the Forest Mother dwells deep in a hidden Cave. As we approached this Sacred Place She emerged to meet us.

"So," She said softly, "it is come at last! Long have I waited for you to find me, my children." The Raven flew down and sat upon Her shoulder, while Brufus loped up to rub against Her legs. The Stag behind the trees bellowed once, and tore up the turf with a huge, ringing hoof, whilst the man stood quite still and gazed long into Her eyes . . . and I? I was afraid, though I knew not, then, what I feared. I hung back behind the man, whom I loved, hoping that the gaze of the Wudu-Maer would not fall upon me.

"You have fasted long," She spoke to the man, "and have drunk and washed in the Waters of Life. You have lived and hunted in my Forest, and have shared life with these, your Companions. Now your Quest is upon you, you who are the Chosen One, and your Destiny awaits you in yonder trees." She gestured towards the Stag. "Will you prevail?" she asked, "or will he?"

The man's eyes widened as he looked from Her to the Stag and back again. "*I'll not fight him!*" he cried.

"Fight him you will!" She replied softly.

With a movement swift and unexpected She stepped forward

and grabbed me where I stood. With a brief gesture, and a murmuring in an unknown tongue, She laid a mighty enchantment upon me, and I howled as I felt my body shift and change. I struggled in Her grip as I realised with horror that I had become another creature, one such as the man — the female of his Kind, woman. He reached for me and cried out my name, but the Wudu-Maer eluded his grasp and dragged me to the trees where the Stag waited still. I fell to the ground before the beast as he bellowed, lowered his vast antlers, and charged!

The man sprang between us with naught but his flint knife in hand. The Stag swung his head wildly then reared to slash with his sharp hooves. Nimbly springing to one side, rolling, then finding his feet again, the man ran for the Forest, the Stag in furious pursuit.

A deathly silence descended on the clearing before the Cave as the sounds of the man and the Stag receded into the Forest. The Forest Mother looked at me sadly.

"I am sorry, Ulrika, to use you thus. The man is young as yet, and his heart is tender. He will fight for *you*, and that will serve my purpose, for in you he sees the Sacred Spirit of the Forest, the very Earth and the Sky above, and Life itself. He is Herne, the Hunter, My beloved Son, Champion of Life and Lord of Death. He is the hunter and the hunted, the slayer and the slain. He is the Traveller who journeys through birth and death and rebirth, just as I and my Cave are the tomb that awaits him and the womb that brings him forth into life." So saying, She laid Her hand upon my human face. "Ah, Ulrika, what have I wrought this day? Wolf you were born and Wolf you must always be, and yet this enchantment, once woven, cannot be undone! Therefore must ye be both Wolf and Woman, Shapechanger, Enchanted One . . . forgive me, Ulrika!"

Evening fell as still we waited, the Wudu-Maer's face tense and still as stone, as we listened . . . and listened . . . and waited. A small fire flickered before the Cave and around it we sat, the Forest Mother with the Raven on Her shoulder and the Bear at

Her feet. I, too, sat close by Her, each moment passing like a year as the night dragged on.

Suddenly we heard a sound, and by the light of the fire we dimly saw a movement in the trees. I gasped in dismay . . . those were antlers I saw! And yet . . . what wonder was this? Striding into the clearing came the familiar figure of the man, and yet it was not him! Or rather it was both him and the God he had become; tall, powerful, alive with the raw energy of Life itself, His head crowned with the antlers of the mighty Horned Hunter. He approached and knelt at the feet of the Forest Mother.

"Mother, Queen, Goddess of All," His deep voice throbbed with passion. "My Quest is victorious, after all — My destiny fulfilled this night! I am become that which was preordained from before the beginning of time! I understand!"

The Wudu-Maer smiled and rose. She turned to me.

"I have taken much from you, Ulrika, and laid much upon your head that you did not seek. I cannot change that which has been done, but I can, at least, give to you this night." Leading the Bear, and carrying the Raven upon Her shoulder, She disappeared into Her Cave, leaving the Chosen One and I, still in Woman-form, alone beneath the Moon . . .

The Sun was soon to rise upon a frosty, silent Forest, the pre-dawn mists weaving a solemn dance amongst the trees. The Wudu-Maer appeared at the mouth of Her Cave, the Cave with no ending that leads deep into the very heart of the Earth to the Underworld beyond. She beckoned. The man followed.

Shimmering into Wolf-form, the better to vent my grief, I raised my nose to the sky and greeted the dawn with a howl of loss, and grief, and pain . . .'

*   *   *

The Circles of Light and Dark

The Power Animals of the Twin Circles

Consider, for a moment, what life could be like both for yourself and for the Planet on which you dwell, if you could see and understand the Patterns of Change in their cyclic entirety, without getting caught up in concepts of Time and Personalisation.

We recommend reflection on the 'circular' rather than the 'linear'; e.g. all things within the known universe revolve around each other in ever-widening Patterns eternally and infinitely; those 'circular' forms can be considered from the greatest in cycle (i.e. to the furthest reaches of universal revolution) to the infinitely small.

One piece of meditation given recently to a group of our students was to give the answer to the following question: when does Zero become One? They went away for the week, and on returning gave me a virtual deluge of 'esoteric' answers. You will be given the answer, of necessity, purely because you cannot go away for a week and come back after consideration of this most simple question (one through which your thoughts will learn new clarity) — one that requires answering in truth — as there can only be one answer — Never! Zero is going to remain Zero forever; One is going to remain One forever — they can only and forever *relate* to each other, they can never *be* each other. If you consider this, meditate and examine, you will probably come to the conclusion that *all* numbers (and they are considered sacred for good reasons, but that is another story) are *possible* when considering Zero and, as such, Zero remains infinitely pregnant with possibility. As there is no such thing as 'nothing' the greatest and the smallest are merely relative to each other and, therefore, reflect each other always.

Light and Dark are to be considered in the same context.

Light could be considered infinite in its possibilities as can Darkness. One can only perceive Light in balance with its opposite; the positive and expansive force of not only your own soul but also that of the universe can only be truly understood if one takes the time to consider the negative and contractive — or the Circles of Light and Dark.

Allow us to make it very clear that the language of Magic, and its ability to evoke *reaction* within the world, as Between-the-Worlds, is that of both Image and Symbol — when a concept is transmuted into either an image or a symbol it takes on a form of 'life' that is not synonymous with the spoken or the written word, unless the word becomes the Word, i.e. a Sigil of the original statement that is summoned to represent what the spoken form could never do. This work, to date, that you are reading will have, hopefully, summoned from within you the images that represent *more* than the work. The spoken Ritual, for example, without the attending visualisations would be a gesture only and would have no validity as a Magical procedure.

So, when performing all 'workings' of an *external nature* — i.e. those that affect your personal world, those that assist you with conscious and inspirational and creative pursuits, that to which you aspire — then the Circle of Light is where and when you will work: the waxing Lunar Cycle (from New Moon to Full); the waxing Solar Year (for long-range projects), which goes from Winter Solstice through to the day prior to the Summer Solstice. When working with Planetary influence you will work when the Planet concerned is *direct* and not when it is retrograde. Consider when Planetary or Stellar influences are at Zenith and not Nadir.

When performing all workings of an *internal nature* — i.e. Shadow work, faults within the self that require upliftment, exploration of the environmental problems that affect the procession of the Cycles (those problems that currently threaten our seasonal tranquillity, such as the Greenhouse Effect), all banishings and bindings — you will work best if accessing the Circle of Dark: the waning Lunar Cycle (from the second day of the Full Moon to the day prior to the New Moon); the waning Solar Year (for long-range projects), which takes you from the Summer Solstice to the day prior to the Winter Solstice; when the Planets are retrograde you can log the effects on not only you personally, but those around you and incidents occurring across the Planet, and the same when Planetary or Stellar influences are at their Nadir.

The research currently being gathered by observation will prove invaluable in perpetuating harmony, and self-evaluation will allow you to remain within your own, disciplined, limitations. These limitations, like Saturn, are merely there as a guidance to personal control — to walk outside your own limitational field without first having acknowledged its conceivable boundary means to lose control, and that will never do! This does not mean that one cannot explore the fullness of emotional, physical, mental or creative potential; it means that within that fullness one creates no harm. If, however, one does not realise one's own limits then one cannot supersede them, if that is what is required, or, like the Tarot Card of the Devil, one can become trapped by them therefore creating unwanted habit-patterns or obsessions.

The Priest and Priestess of Magic cannot afford *not* to work at Saturn's Gate!

The Power Animals are archetypal *allies*. You will summon Them.

You will work at summoning Them in your Ritual Circle at the times indicated above.

The purpose of summoning Them is to invoke Their essence for both the strength and the gifts that only the Wild Ones can impart.

It is the understanding and the qualities that you must seek to invoke and absorb when Ritually working with these Wild Ones. To assist you with this work you must first allow the force of these Beings to influence you, and then, whilst still in your Circle, work at the perfection of your Book of Elements by recording your personal observations during the Ritual.

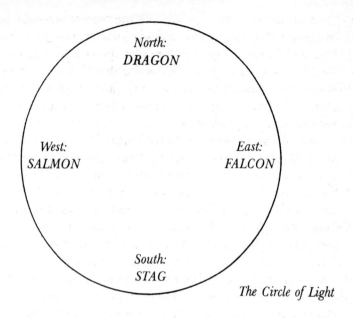

The Circle of Light

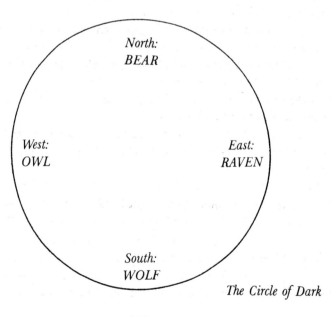

The Circle of Dark

If you are working the *Circle of Light* you will record those parts of yourself that are associated with the corresponding Element: you are to acknowledge your 'best' aspects!

If you are working the *Circle of Dark* you will record those parts of yourself that are associated with the corresponding Element: you are to acknowledge your 'worst' aspects!

Be wary, however, of gauging either your 'best' or your 'worst' by conditioned standards, as many of the standards of our culture are concerned with the denial of our strengths, the repression of our free speech, the unacceptability of our desired fulfilments if they do not conform with the traditionally acceptable (usually stemming from the religious ethics of those not of our Path).

Australia, at this period of history, is making enormous breakthroughs in both the scientific and medical fields, its scholastic levels are excellent, its Arts are world standard, we are known for our sense of humour and our flexibility, but we are still very much in the grip of fear and ignorance where the Occult is concerned, and the media does little but compare our Paths to 'devil worship', tending to lump everything under one banner. Many have said that we stick our necks out just going to print, but Life is given to us, along with the ability to reason, so that we may do with it as we Will (e'er it harm none).

So, you work at the blocks in your life by confronting, through your Training, your greatest possibilities and your deepest fears.

To do so without the aid of the Forces beyond the Veil would tend to be a near-impossible task. The Paths we tread have been travelled for eternity and the signs along the way are well set — those available through the minds of those who have shared through the spoken and/or written word, and those that are available through accessing contact with the Inner Ones.

Keeping Records

There are four Books that you will have to acquire, two unlined and two lined, and as time passes you will just keep on collecting information and references and will end up with a veritable library of accumulated notes and information. This process is a necessary one insofar as much of the important work of Occultists in the past has been lost or destroyed, to the detriment of future seekers along the same Path.

You may seek to study the Magical systems of Celtic origin or Egyptian Magic, of the Graeco-Romans or those of the Middle East, the Amerindian ways, other Shamanic traditions, the Norse traditions, to name a few. You will find yourself stimulated by certain traditions more than others, but however you go about perfecting your own Path you will find yourself studying the histories of these people and their religious and Magical inheritances. You may find yourself, as a matter of course, studying Herbalism, Naturopathics or any of the healing Arts; there is Tarot, Qabbalah, Astrology, Geomancy, Numerology, Hermetics, Alchemy. You may seek to understand the ways of our Western culture by looking at Christianity, both philosophically and historically (where you will see that the twain do not meet!), you may take peeks at Astronomy, Physics. You will read and read and read. You will seek to specialise in your own chosen field of inquiry. You may seek to research and explore one of the thousands of offshoots currently available to you through the rising tide of spiritual awareness.

You may seek to discover these things alone and work as a solitary, or you may seek to share yourself with others.

However you do it or wherever your studies lead you, you will need to keep records.

The Book of Shadows
This will be like your personal bible of Rituals. You may take the Rituals that others have worked on and perfected and use them for yourself, and may not ever seek to write your own. However, you *must* personalise them so that they really 'fit' your true allegiances. You will need to seek out the Rites of Moon — Esbat (Full Moon), New Moon, Dark Moon, or wherever you work Ritual in honour of the Moon Goddess; there are the Fire Festivals of Samhain, Feast of Bride, Beltaen and Llughnassad; the Solar Rituals of Solstice and Equinox may need your personal touch; any of the Magical Rituals for whatever reasons that are important; summonings and invocations that work; Sigil Magic; bindings and Rites of recoil, etc.

The Grimoir
Your Book of Correspondences. This Book is invaluable when you work with certain formulae for specific reasons — the hours of the day or night that you work; Incense mixes for specific purposes; what oils or oil blends to use, why and when; all manner of Magical 'recipes' that succeed.

Your Magical Diary
All Inner Plane workings; their results; Contacts and what They tell you; you will record the workings that succeed; pertinent dreams; explorations and experiments.

The Book of Elements
You record your personal observations of yourself, attitudes, wholistic perceptions of others in general.

There are as many reasons for keeping records as you could imagine, and it will prove worthwhile to you and to those serious people with whom you may wish to share (and later, maybe, even to train).

The Ethics of Personal Power

Right at the start of your training and seeking you will need to establish a Pattern of ethics that you *must* stick to. You are entering, or have entered, into a Path that will keep you questing for the rest of your life. There will be no let-up. There is never a walking-away from this Path once your feet are firmly upon it, as it will continue to feed and inspire you; and just about everything ends up being 'looked at' through the eyes of your Path as, once you have sought to understand and be at one with the work of the Evolving Whole, to simply get up in the morning, go to work, go home and go to bed and occasionally socialise will be, for you, the least of worthwhile activity unless it is flavoured with the vitality of Magic.

'Like Attracts Like' is also a certainty. You will come into contact with others of the same or similar Paths with whom you can share and synthesize — these like-minded individuals can become an important focus for love and trust, and it is a shame when that love and trust falls down because the ethics were not established at the onset of the relationship between you.

The ability to abuse the Forces with which you are working has been exploited before, and the ego is always the reason why. Again this could be considered as conditioned response, as we are brought up in an environment of competition — the seeking of power for its own sake being one of the wrong reasons for accessing this Path. Some people will seek knowledge for what it will 'get' them, which is, eventually, nothing. The truest reason for seeking knowledge is firstly to become that which your soul knows you can become, which is a Vessel for that knowledge on the behalf of the Gods.

It is not necessary to acquire, for example, the most fancy Ritual regalia. It is not necessary to wear the fanciest of Robes — when people set out to accumulate just for the sake of how impressive they appear, others of the same Path will become wary as to the reasons why this is being done. Always remember that it is *who* you are, the *direction* of what you learn, and the *Application* of knowledge that are to be your aims: the seeking to perfect your part in the process of continuum — 'Quality is not relative to Quantity' in the Occult Arts.

In the course of balancing your Self to your Gods the following may be of assistance:

Awareness Do not miss anything. In all your undertakings have your six senses working at their fullest potential; this is necessary in both your Magical and your personal life.

Preparation The preparation required of you when working your Path is to be performed with the idea of perfection in mind. If you are preparing a Sacred Space in which to work then you must seek to personalise the entire process by saying: 'Is this the best I can do?' As your Awareness can assist you in being Prepared for whatever is the next stage of the work, so the Preparation is a necessary function of Intent.

Intent Know, at all times, why you are doing what you are doing. There is no reason to set up a Ritual Circle or cleanse with intent of purification unless there is an Intent. That Intent can be as simple as seeking meditation for the purpose of aligning the self with the Self, or it can be as complex as a Qabbalistic Mass — it matters not if your Intent is unclear. And the lack of Intent will doom the work to failure — you may have forgotten something crucial along the way that is of paramount importance if any of the three mentioned thus far are left out or forgotten.

Focus This is a little hard to describe; it is a process obtained when you link emotion and mind into one function. It does not allow anything to interfere. It does not lose control at important moments. It does not allow the mind or the heart to act independently of the purpose at hand. It is almost like 'bearing down' when birthing a child, so controlled is the function, without seeming to be so.

Personal Power This is a natural growth process that develops from the 'work' that you do. Others notice you even when you do not desire it — therefore Personal Power is the ability to 'disappear' when you want to and 'appear' when you want to. It is not an expression of ego — it is a presence about yourself that you will probably need to keep close control of. It will emanate from your aura and is similar to a magnet. This field is not a conscious function and should not be treated as such. Personal Power is a direct result of working Magic, and if you allow yourself to become 'glamoured' by it, in either yourself or anyone else, you create a disservice and abuse of the Forces with which you work — almost like saying 'I am God' or 'I am the Goddess' instead of 'My God works through me' or 'My Goddess works through me'. Personal Power is an accumulation of Awareness, Preparation, Intent and your ability to Focus all three through the Vessel of the Self.

Service Do not confuse the expression with the idea of servitude. You owe Service to the Forces with whom you work. This is an acknowledged outcome to Initiation and you must be prepared to acknowledge the fact that, consciously, there are greater powers at work, wholist-ically, than any individual part. Your Service is in the truth of that which you perpetuate and the need to be 'on call' when you are directed by the Forces that you honour. They will never ask of you anything that will create harm (if, by chance, through lack of any of the above, you come into contact with a presence that is Lower Astral, or Qliphothic, in nature then you will most assuredly know it, for it will desire (a) to fulfil your egoistic desires, and/or (b) request that you go against the principle of 'Do as ye Will, e'er it harm none'), and a thorough banishing and cleansing will take the laxness out of your ineptitude.

You must work at the dispelling of that which you fear. You must seek to be unattached to outcomes or doom yourself to taking on a martyr complex. You may have set ideas about what you think will provide happiness, and this may be a false focus. You are just going to have to trust those Forces of your Path when they send you where you may not wish, consciously, to go; when you meet certain people that you may not, consciously, wish to meet; when They decide that your stability needs an experiential shake-up. At all times, when these events happen, you must seek to understand *why* without necessarily questioning the process — this will, in retrospect, become obvious. You most certainly must work with the expression 'Your Gods will not barter', as They will not — no matter how you moan. Personal gain may not come to you in material form; that is a human form of response. The universe does not necessarily work with the need for payment for services rendered in goods!

Understanding yourself is the first Key. Seeking to align opposites is the second Key. It is the heights to which your spirit can soar that you can seek — and this will not be denied you.

Part Three:
Three Dawns in a Day

The Three Main Functions of the Solar/Earth Priest

We are focusing, in this section, on the three main functions, or directions, of the Solar/Earth Priesthood, but firstly allow us to make clear that even though the functions are known as Degrees, they are not representative of ascending grade as is usual in the established Magical groups; they are 'Deepenings' and your alliance will eventually be with one or more of the three.

1st Degree Priesthood

The growth processes that are achieved through this Degree are reflected through acknowledgement of the Earth as Supreme Provider.

This Degree opens the Priest to the Earth Energies that affect us and that we are effected by. Most of the Rituals in this book are associated with the 1st Degree.

Other than the personal interaction that you will undertake with the Elemental Forces that protect our Planet, with the Faces of God that are associated with Earth Energy and with the attending disciplines, you may find that you will tap into this Force through creative association by way of your Ritual Tools and the understanding of the many processes necessary in the making of them.

Other areas of undertaking are currently held by certain Priests who choose, after fully understanding the 'Deepenings', to work in the capacity of healers, herbalists, husbandmen, ecologists and environmentalists.

Their symbol is the Pentacle.

The *Primum Mobile* of the 1st Degree Priest is the *Green Ray*.

2nd Degree Priesthood
Those Priests who have come to fully understand their interconnectedness to the Earth and the energies that support life, here, in all its diverse aspects, will proceed to learn of the Mysteries through the legends and mythologies of their chosen Path. They may choose to look at the psychological implication of archetypal analogy, the effects of Magic in the consciousness, etc.

They are the Wayshowers who choose to teach others in the various capacities already existing in standard Occult practices. They work the Rites to the Earth, Moon, Sun and Stars and work their training through the Line of the Merlyn; they are the Musicians, the Poets, the Talkers and Storytellers, the Writers, the Artists who express to others by way of both art and science. They find themselves within the framework of modern society and often choose to remain in standard occupations or lifestyles, whilst still working their Craft and creating their Art.

Many of the Priesthood choose to return to this Degree after the Deepening and remain to specialise.

Their symbol is the Staff.

The *Primum Mobile* of the 2nd Degree Priest is the *Red Ray*.

3rd Degree Priesthood
The Priests who have come to learn of the Great Earth as Provider, and who have come to learn of the Rites and Rituals of their Priesthood and the Myths and Mysteries of their Line, will come to the Thresholds and remain Between-the-Worlds.

Here is the Priest of the Inner Mysteries, who seeks to invoke the very Essence of their Gods into themselves for the specific task of influencing the course of the Evolving Whole through the *honour* of the Evolving Whole — honour being the foundation stone (the Lia Fal) of them all. They are the Star-seed, their purpose purely to serve the Forces of Revolution (which, in esoteric terms, has to do with the overall Patterns of Change). They are the Walkers of the Inner Planes, and their Temples, whilst being 'earthed' in our known dimension, have their parallels in not only Gwynvyd but also Ceugant.

They are the Priests of Llugh, the Lance; the Warriors of Light; the Champions of the Goddess.

They will dare to be different, will move out of mainstream lifestyles and will seek to re-establish the Plane of the High Gods and Goddesses upon the Earth through Magic and Invocation.

They are the teachers of the Priesthood of the Green and Red Lines, as well as the passers-on of re-established links with the ancient past to those who have learned and sought to work their Path in the *now*.

Their symbol is the Sword.

The *Primum Mobile* of the 3rd Degree Priest is the *Black Line*.

So it is, also, with the Priestesses of Magic, but after another fashion.

All are Grail Seekers.

The Evolving Whole

This expression has occurred many times in this work, so, in the fashion of the work so far, I will begin this passage with yet another story!

Some may find offence with certain parts of the story and for this I make no apology. The culture within which we learn and gain our understandings of both history and religion has guided us away from our very beautiful inheritance for long enough, until the truth of it has been distorted, ridiculed and, of a consequence, almost (but not quite) lost.

The destruction of one's tribal and spiritual inheritance is a blatant act of brutality — for the truth is that the people who sought to hold to their beliefs and legends *were* killed! The knowledge that was written down *was* decimated! The so-called 'heretics' *were* annihilated! And no religion or government *ever* has that right!

* * *

The Spinning Wheel

I want to tell you a Story . . .

This Story has no beginning and no end . . .

Not yet anyway.

There is still time to stop the Story ending; for if it was done, if it were to end, it would not be a Story but a travesty, and an ending could do nothing but mock the Story.

There is a Palingenetic Inheritance within the soul and body of every one of us that we cannot help but feel . . . and so we search, to find our spirit in strange lands and in other peoples' faith and in other passages.

No wonder that we yearn yet!

For in the blood of many of us there dwells the Seed of Legend.

I tell the Story of the Spinning Wheel.

'Once upon a time a Woman stood upon the Mountain-Beyond-Time. The Mountain was of Darkness and She understood Its Depths. There She stood, Her body arching into the Void like a curve of Light within eternal Night.

She was alone.

Within Her belly was a gnawing emptiness that would not fill. She knew it should not feel that way and could not ease the emptiness alone.

She called from within Herself a Sound.

It issued from Her mouth in Power and Strength and Beauty and, like the peal of millions of bells, it rang out and across the Darkness seeking, seeking . . . seeking an answer. The vibration of Her call was so powerful that the Mountain-Beyond-Time upon which She stood began to rumble in reply.

The vibration of Her call was so strong that the Mountain-Beyond-Time began to break up beneath Her feet.

The vibration of Her call was so beautiful that the Mountain-Beyond-Time was inspired to take from within Itself a Soul, as it shattered into an infinite plethora of crystal Star-shapes.

Into the far reaches of Eternity did They soar, each particle alive with the glory of Her call, Her Song; each breaking forth again and again into countless billions of living Suns that fed from the Breast of the Woman-of-Darkness and became Whole.

They so loved Who They were and from Whence They came that They Danced in ever-widening Spirals and Patterns . . .
Each One unique.
Each One aware, with a common Soul and a myriad of spirit,
of Each Other and the Order of Their lives,
and the nurturing of Their Mother,
Who is Space,
Through Which All is born;
Who is the Great Sea, Outside-of-Time.

The Woman-Outside-of-Time was aware of what She had done and loved the Dancers of the Wheel, and they loved the Voice of the Singer Who brought Them forth.

Many of the Dancers sought within the Great Soul a way to give more of Themselves in honour of the Singer Who called the Song, and so They merged with Her in a Greater Love than had been known to Her Mother Who is the Void and Her Father Who is the Mountain-Outside-of-Time. And so the Stars and the Vault of the Sky, Who had brought Them into Being, bore forth the Earths, one after the other, throughout Eternity . . .
Each One was unique.
Each One aware,
With a common Soul and a myriad of spirit,
of each Other and the Order of Their lives,
and the nurturing of Their Mother,
Who is Space,
Through which All is born;
Who is the Great Sea, Outside-of-Time.

And in one small part of the Pattern, in one small Place-Within-Time, amongst all this glory and singing and dancing, was a Father Sun so in Love with the Daughter Earth that Danced like a Jewel of blues and greens around Him that He said:
"I do love Thee for all time, I shall gently shine for Thee that Thou might bear Children of Thine own, that the Spiral Dance should never cease, and together shall we love, to spin the Web of the Singer and Dance the joy of the Dance!"

And so the Pattern formed.
And so within every Stone and Flame and Drop of Water and Blade of Grass and Leaf and Fruit and Flower and Child of Wing and Child of Fur, of Blood and Bone and Fin and Leg, within *all* that lived existed the Pattern . . .
Of the Knowledge of the Singer of the Song,
Of the Dancers of the Dance.

And upon the Islands of the Earth's Seas the People knew
. . .
They Sang and Danced and shared in the Pattern and honoured
It
and called it a Goddess and called it a God . . .
And the Singer saw and She said:
   "O Father Sun of this little paradise, I seek to have the
Creatures like Me and I seek to have the Creatures like You so
that They can Love!"

And so They were divided . . . into Female did She see Herself
reflected . . . and so They Sang.
Into Male did She see Her Lovers reflected . . . and so They
Danced.
And They shared with each other the gifts of Song and Dance,
and there was also love!
They were born, They lived, They died; Plant and Animal and
Stone and Sea; changing, ever-changing, fulfilling the Pattern.
And they Understood . . .
And the Singer saw and said:
   "Brother Sun and Father of My Children do I give to Thee a
Great and Holy Lover! Thou hast fulfilled Me as I have fulfilled
Thee — and Mine is ever to give and give and give!"

She gave to Her Son the Sun and Her Daughter the Earth the
Whole and Continuous One . . . the Absolute Spirit of herself
that lit the Sky at Midnight with Silver Light of Wonder and
Mystery . . . the Moon Who is Goddess of our Darkness. Her
Pattern was that of Woman and the deep tidal Mystery of the
Waters and those that rise and fall in all the Earth's Blood, from
Oceans and Rain to the Body of Woman and the Mind of each
thing including the Spirit of Man.

And the Sun and Moon Sing Their Song and Dance Their own
Dance . . . so it has of old been known!

And the Daughters of the Holy Mother are the Women of the

Earth, who Know each other always. And the Sons of the Sun are the Men of the Earth who Know each other always. And within each Woman there dwells a Priestess of the Ancient Mysteries if only she would look; within men there dwells a Priest of the Dance if only he would seek.

Within us now is an Island . . . around the Island is a Lake; it has passed into the Mists of the Mind of the Whole and dwells there waiting . . .

Not for a Key, not even for Knowledge, but for Belief. For the Dreamer who dares to break the rule of lock and chain and who seeks to Dance with Morgan-le-Fey; who seeks to Sing of Possibilities!

Within the Lake is a Sword that was sent within its depths by the hand of a man who felt his Power failing in the face of those who created a wrathful god who sought to divide women from men, nation from nation, spirit from spirit — the men in black who worship at the feet of a constant Death, who condemn the Dancers of the Dance and the Singers of the Song and who tell the People that their trapped and burdened god is all there is! They condemned the Pattern and called it 'evil' and seduced the People with promise of domination (and the threat of damnation!).

And the Mistress of the Waters took the Sword within the Lake and readied Herself to wait the long wait . . .

For She knew, as He knew, but could not stop, the wars that came and the pain and the loss — the rape of spirit, the eating-up of the Earth Mother's Flesh and the power over others through Fear!

But the Legend lives . . .

> They so loved Who They were,
> And from Whence They came,
> that They Danced in ever-widening Spirals and Patterns,
> Each One unique,
> Each One aware,

With a common Soul and a myriad of spirit,
of each other and the Order of Their lives,
and the nurturing of Their Mother,
Who is Space,
Through which *all* is born;
Who is the Great Sea, Outside-of-Time . . .

And within us all we remember . . .
The Singer Who Sings the Song;
The Dancers Who Dance the Dance;
And the ever turning,
Life fulfilling,
Majesty of the Wheel!'

*   *   *

Notes on Human Nature

The most important aspect of a well trained Priest or Priestess is the acquisition of Balance. There are four sides to the nature of people.

1. The bright, laughing, joyous side, the side we have been taught, in our culture, to honour, to seek to show to the world; the side that is 'at peace'. And it is not fulfilled.

2. The 'questor'; the one that seeks to change what is immediately recognised as 'limiting' — this side of our nature is concerned with what is on the 'outside'. It is the side that seeks to imprint our very existence on both other people and our environment. And it is not fulfilled.

3. The third side is all mixed up with learning and patterns, understanding, creativity and curiosity — it is a very brave side — but it is not fulfilled.

4 The 'dark' side, or our shadow-selves; this side, in our culture, we are taught is a wrongness; it is to be controlled, suppressed, destroyed; it is 'evil' and 'dangerous' — so we seek to fulfil the other three and deny the fourth and, as a consequence, it is a Dragon within us! All our pain, both physical and emotional; all our 'dead-ends', our unresolved angers and our futilities pour down the tunnel of our shadow-selves and stay there! The person who has not been touched by hurt is not lucky, he is defenceless, or he is lying.

It is our Wild Side.

Also, as anyone who has known pain will tell you, it is the most powerful side, as within it resides not only all our experiences that have hurt, but our racial and instinctual memories, our attachment to the Collective Unconscious, our ability to perpetuate the first three on the list, our ability to survive — even our will to live; our ability to protect as well as to procreate and perpetuate; our sense of one-ness with our Planet and those things upon the Planet that have not yet been tamed or subdued or destroyed by man, like mountains, the forests, oceans, wind, rain, fire, weeds, wild animals and birds and creatures of the oceans, bugs and even disease — the biggest, the wildest, the most utterly untamable being death.

We are intelligent, but we are also wild.

The necessity to acknowledge this and then to take hold of it with mind, body and soul is your Path to deeper Knowledge.

Epilogue

'For man is ever a star, and woman a moon . . . '

The Stone Circle stands silent and watchful upon the empty moor. As the day draws to a close, the signs of Summer, subtle as they are in this windswept place, can be seen, felt and heard all around.

The Sun dips closer and closer towards the western horizon, creating mysterious depths and hollows within the Circle of still-warm Stones as They cast Their shadows long upon the ground. At first glance the Circle seems empty, its stillness unbroken, its brooding inner power thrumming quietly within itself. Yet, as we look more closely, the figure of a man can be seen as still as the Stones Themselves, standing facing the Setting Sun. At the moment of the Sun's disappearance, in a glory of golden light in a crimson sky, the man raises his arms and begins a low, strong, beautiful chant. The words he uses we know not, yet the power, respect, love and a strange yearning too, are unmistakable.

Darkness now hastens to claim Her time, as the light fades into dusk and the man turns to face inwards into the Circle to bring the Sunset Ritual to a close.

Would that we could read his thoughts, you say, and understand the sad and haunted light behind his calm, steady gaze. Ah, 'tis fortunate indeed that you are here now, and the more fortunate still that you be permitted to stay, and watch.

The Priest pauses a moment before he moves to close the Circle and conclude his worship. The Night has almost fully fallen, and once again the by now familiar feelings of loss and loneliness stir faintly, yet relentlessly, behind the iron-strong hand of discipline he holds upon his heart. The worship of the Sun, Lord of Light and Life, the Divine Fire of Inspiration and the Creative Force of his Universe, is the whole of his life and his soul's spark burns steadily in Its Flame.

By the light of Day does he know his place and his Path, by the readiness of the Sun does he Dance the Dance of Creation and know he the steps in perfect time to the rhythm and the heat of Life. And then comes the Night, and with it come the unnamed yearnings and the pain of loss and the seeking for completion. And yes, let us be naught but honest, with the Night come also the secret, hidden fears.

The Moon is rising now, above the Sacred Stone that by Day is the Altar to the Sun, and casts Her silver glow into the Circle. The familiar scene becomes unearthly and filled with Mystery as the man stands and watches the play of Light and Dark, shining and shadowed upon the Stones. This is the time when he would normally leave, leaving the Shrine to the Dark and haunted Night, until his time should come again.

Yet tonight he remains — motionless, watchful, waiting. His heart beats just a little faster, just a little harder, as the Presence within the Stones grows stronger. Eventually, within the deep shadows beside a far Stone he discerns a figure. A small and delicate figure it is, Robed, it would seem, from the swirling Darkness Itself. A darkening and a thickening of the shadows, and as black as the deepest, sunless sky.

The figure steps forward into the Circle and the Priest of the Sun sees that it is, indeed, a woman, though whether mortal or not he cannot tell. Through a mixture of wonderment, longing and personal fear he asks: 'Who are you?'

She smiles and moves, and within the dark folds of her cloak tiny, brilliant points of light shine and twinkle like stars in an endless sky. Her voice is soft in reply: 'I have no name for what it is that I am, or what it is that I do, only do I know that it is shaped of Darkness. I am the hidden depths of Night, and the Moon among Stars. I am the spinning Vortex of Infinity. I am Silence, and Patience, and Stillness. I am the dark Womb and the dark Tomb and we are one. I am the bare bones of all that is, and I am the Force that crumbles them to dust, and the Darkness that claims them. I am the quiet stone and the rich, damp soil beneath your feet. I am the mystery of the deep, still Pool. *I* am the longing and the hunger within your soul. I am the Grail that holds the Wine of Life; drink deeply of me, Priest of the Sun, and know the taste of me upon your lips. Stay with me, Lord, as I tread the steps of the Dance of Darkness, so that I may feel the honour you bring me — as *I* will stay when the Night is done, hidden in the shadows, secret and still, and bring homage and help to your side. Alone you and I have stood in this Place, and to each has been a time and a purpose. Now shall we then stand together, so that your purpose shall be as mine, and mine as yours? For there is *no* day without night, and one must ever give way to the other! Herein lies the Mystery! The Lord shall ever yearn for His Lady, and She will ever seek Him out.'

This is the nature of ourselves, and our Priesthood — Priest and Priestess of Magic . . .

'For we are the Mirror of the Whole . . .'

Recommended Reading List

Non-Fiction

Ashcroft-Nowicki, Dolores. *First Steps in Ritual*, Aquarian Press, Wellingborough, UK. New edn 1990.

Ashcroft-Nowicki, Dolores. (Ed.) *The Forgotten Mage*, Aquarian Press, Wellingborough, UK, 1986.

Ashcroft-Nowicki, Dolores. *Ritual Magic Workbook*, Aquarian Press, Wellingborough, UK, 1986.

Ashcroft-Nowicki, Dolores. *The Shining Paths*, Aquarian Press, Wellingborough, UK, 1983.

Cooper, J.C. *An Illustrated Encyclopaedia of Traditional Symbols*, Thames & Hudson, London. New edn 1979.

Crowley, A. *Magick*, Samuel Weiser Inc., Me, USA, 1973.

de Chardin, T. *The Future of Man*, Harper & Row, New York, 1969.

Denning, M. & Phillips, O. *The Sword and the Serpent*, Llewellyn Publications, Minnesota, 1987.

Drury, Nevill. *The Occult Experience*, Robert Hale Ltd, London, 1987.

Farrar, S. & J. *Eight Sabbats for Witches,* Robert Hale, Ltd, London, 1981

Frazer, J. *The Golden Bough*, McMillan, London. 13 Vols, 1936.

Graves, R. *The White Goddess*, Farrar, Strauss & Giroux, New York, 1966.

Gray, W.G. *The Ladder of Lights*, Helios Books UK, 1958.

Green, M. *Magic for the Aquarian Age*, Aquarian Press, Wellingborough, UK, 1983.

Hall, N. *The Moon and the Virgin*, Harper & Row, New York, 1981.

Hartley, Christine. *The Western Mystery Tradition*, Aquarian Press, Wellingborough, UK, 1986.

Jung, C. *The Archetypes and the Collective Unconscious*, Vol I. Princeton University Press, New Jersey, USA.

Knight, Gareth. *Secret Tradition in Arthurian Legend*, Aquarian Press, Wellingborough, UK, 1983.

Knight, Gareth. *A Practical Guide to Qabbalistic Symbolism,*, Helios Books UK, 1966.

Lethbridge, T.C. *Gogmagog*, Routledge & Kegan Paul, London, 1957.

Matthews, John and Caitlin. *The Western Way* Vols 1 and 2. Arcana, London 1986.

Matthews, John and Caitlin. *Mabon*, Arcana, London, 1990.

Regardie, Israel. *The Golden Dawn*, Llewellyn Publications, Minnesota, 1974.

Regardie, Israel. *Garden of Pomegranates*, Llewellyn Publications, Minnesota, 1985.

Richardson, Alan. *Gate of Moon*, Aquarian Press, Wellingborough, UK, 1984.

Richardson, Alan. *Introduction to the Mystical Qabbalah*, Aquarian Press, Wellingborough, UK. Paths to Inner Power series, 1987.

Richardson, Alan and Hughes, Geoff. *Ancient Magicks for a New Age*, Llewellyn Publications, Minnesota, 1989.

Spence, Lewis. *The Myths of Ancient Egypt*, G.G. Harrap, London, 1915.

Spence, Lewis. *The Magic Arts in Celtic Britain*, Ryder & Co., London & New York, 1945.

Squire, Charles. *Celtic Myth and Legend*, Greshan Publishers, London, 1905.

Starhawk. *Dreaming the Dark*, Beacon Press, Boston, 1982.

Stone, Merlin. *When God was a Woman*, Virago Press, London, 1976.

Sturzaker, James. *Kabbalistic Aphorisms*, Metatron UK. 2nd edn, 1981.

Valiente, Doreen. *Where Witchcraft Lives*, Aquarian Press, Wellingborough, UK, 1962.

Walker, B.G. *The Women's Encyclopedia of Myths and Secrets*, Harper & Row, New York, 1983.

Warren-Clarke, Ly. *The Way of the Goddess*, Prism/Unity Press, Bridport, UK, 1987.

Fiction

Bradley, Marion. *Mists of Avalon*, Sphere Books, London, 1984.

Flint, Kenneth. *Challenge of the Clans*, Bantam Press, London, 1987.

Flint, Kenneth. *Champion of the Sidhe*, Bantam Press, London, 1986.

Flint, Kenneth. *Riders of the Sidhe*, Bantam Press, London, 1987.

Fortune, Dion. *The Sea Priestess*, Aquarian Press, Wellingborough, UK. New edn, 1989.

Howard, Robert E. *The Sign of the Moonbow*, Berkley Publishing, New York, 1977.

Paxson, Diana L. *The White Raven*, Avon Books, New York, 1989.